RELIGIOUS LIBERTY IN THE AMERICAN REPUBLIC

D1403658

© 2008 by The Heritage Foundation
214 Massachusetts Avenue, NE
Washington, DC 20002-4999
202.546.4400 • *heritage.org*

Printed in the United States of America

ISBN: 978-0-89195-131-5
Cover photo by Will Brown

The cover illustration depicts a stained-glass panel located at Christ Church in Philadelphia that commemorates the first prayer in the First Continental Congress on September 7, 1774. Those gathered in the Congress offered this prayer to invoke Divine Providence to grant them wisdom and protection in the coming struggle against the British Empire. The Reverend Jacob Duche of Christ Church led the prayer at the invitation of the assembly. John Adams reported to his wife Abigail that "I must confess I never heard a better prayer, or one so well pronounced. ... It has had an excellent effect upon everybody here."

RELIGIOUS LIBERTY IN THE AMERICAN REPUBLIC

By Gerard V. Bradley

TABLE OF CONTENTS

PREFACE

We are often told that religion is divisive and ought to be kept away from politics, and that religious liberty means a strict separation of church and state, but that view is out of tune with the proper understanding of the role that religion and morality play in the civic and public life of a self-governing people. A more compelling model is that of America's Founders, who advanced religious liberty in a way that would uphold religion and morality as indispensable supports of good habits, the firmest props of the duties of citizens, and the great pillars of human happiness.

Many different peoples came to the British colonies to flee religious persecution, seeking to escape the religious battles that had bloodied the European continent. The American Founders sought to prevent those divisions from spreading to the New World.

But far from wanting to expunge religion from public life, the Founders encouraged religion as a necessary and vital part of their new nation. They sought the official separation of church and state in order to build civil and religious liberty on the grounds of equal natural rights and the consent of the governed, but they never intended—indeed, they roundly rejected—the idea of separating religion and politics.

Church doctrine would not determine the laws, and laws would not determine church doctrine. Yet they favored government encouragement and support of religion in public laws, in official speeches and ceremonies, on public property and in public buildings, and even in public schools.

The Founders' support for blending religion and politics was based on the following syllogism: Morality is necessary for republican government; religion is necessary for morality; therefore, religion is necessary for republican government. "Of all the dispositions and habits which lead to political prosperity," Washington wrote in his Farewell Address, "Religion and morality are indispensable supports. In vain would that man claim the tribute of Patriotism who should labor to subvert these great Pillars of human happiness—these firmest props of the duties of Men and citizens."

In the end, while it is often thought that religion and politics must be discussed as if they are radically separate spheres, the Founders' conception of religious liberty was almost exactly the opposite. It actually requires the *moralization* of politics, which includes—and requires—the continuing influence of religion in public life.

The health of liberty depends on the principles, standards, and morals common to all religions. By acknowledging the realm in which reason and faith agree and can cooperate about morality and politics, religious liberty unites civic morality and the moral teachings of religion, thereby establishing common standards to guide private and public life. At the same time it reminds man to pursue his transcendent duties and frees religion to pursue its divine mission among men.

As Alexis de Tocqueville observed in *Democracy in America*, even though religion "never intervenes directly in the government of American society," it nevertheless determines the "habits of the heart" and is "the first of their political institutions." The result is that, throughout American history, religion has flourished—and so has liberty.

Preface

Observing various ethical and social problems in modern American society, it is clear that these ills have arisen not *because* we have followed the wisdom of the Founders, but largely because we have *ignored* it. Rebuilding a post–welfare state society demands the return of religion and faith-based institutions to their central role in the nation's civic and public life.

To attain this, Americans must abandon the interpretation—maintained by the Supreme Court—that religion is in conflict with freedom and that any "endorsement" of religion creates an unconstitutional religious establishment. That interpretation wrongly and unwisely prevents government from recognizing or advancing religious faith generally.

In this monograph, Gerard Bradley explains the Founders' view of the relationship between religion and politics and demonstrates how the Supreme Court deviated from this view in embarking on a project aimed at the secularization of American politics and society. In doing so, Bradley reveals the naked prejudices of many of these Supreme Court justices, as well as the shoddy jurisprudence upon which their most radical decisions have been based.

Professor Bradley is eminently qualified to make this case. He is a professor of law at the University of Notre Dame; a noted scholar in the areas of constitutional law, religion, and public life; and author of the acclaimed book *Church–State Relationships in America*. In addition to his professorship at Notre Dame, he currently serves as director of the Witherspoon Institute's Center on Religion and the Constitution and chairman of the Federalist Society's Religious Liberties Practice Group. His distinguished career has focused on the question of the intersection between religion and politics in America. Joseph Postell contributed to editing this monograph, and he and Julia Shaw are responsible for the case descriptions.

This publication is part of a series of occasional essays and booklets published by The Heritage Foundation, under the auspices of the B. Kenneth Simon Center for American Studies, on the "First Principles" of the American tradition of ordered liberty that we seek to conserve "for ourselves and our posterity," as it says in our Constitution. Publications cover a range of themes and topics, each aimed at explaining our most primary ideas—ideas that often have been forgotten or rejected—and considering what those principles should mean for America today.

The series is motivated by a powerful observation: Those who lead our nation today—and those who will lead it tomorrow—must *know* and *understand* our first principles if they mean to vindicate those principles and see to it that they once again guide our country.

Today, two related developments are challenging the secularization of American politics that occurred under the direction of the Supreme Court in the 20th century. On the one hand, the cultural decline encouraged by the Court's secularization project has produced a strong backlash among the American people, who support the idea of government promoting religion in a non-discriminatory manner in the process of governing. At the same time, even as the Court has tried to moderate its secular jurisprudence, it has also impinged upon religious freedom by discriminating *against* religious groups as a result of confused Establishment Clause jurisprudence.

A sober view of these problematic effects, combined with a proper understanding of the history of religious liberty illustrated here by Gerard Bradley, should encourage all of us to defend the basic principle that government and religion can and must partner together if we are going to secure the blessings of liberty—including especially our religious freedom—for future generations.

Matthew Spalding
Director, B. Kenneth Simon Center for American Studies
First Principles Series Editor

INTRODUCTION

*T*he federal Constitution—the charter of our national government since 1789—makes few references to religion. The Constitution bans religious tests for national political office. The First Amendment, which was ratified in 1791, forbids "laws respecting an establishment of religion." It guarantees "free exercise" to everyone.

Americans have always been an extraordinarily religious people too. They have characteristically held tight to their faiths; held that the faith of an individual makes one (largely) the person that one is; and held that the faith of the nation makes us the people we are. As the Supreme Court famously said in 1952, "We are a religious people whose institutions presuppose a Supreme Being."[1]

Americans have also characteristically relied on their religious faith to help them understand America's role in the world—as a beacon of light, as "a city upon a hill," as a "redeemer nation," as a nation whose conduct both depends upon and fulfills a Providential plan for humankind. As the Supreme Court wrote in 1963 (even as it held that devotional Bible readings in public schools were unconstitutional), "It can be truly said, therefore, that today, as in the beginning, our national life reflects a religious people who, in the words of James Madison, are 'earnestly praying, as...in duty bound,

---

[1.] *Zorach v. Clausen*, 343 U.S. 306, 313 (1952).

I

that the Supreme Lawgiver of the Universe...guide them into every measure which may be worthy of his [blessing...]."[2]

Throughout their history, the people of the United States have welcomed diverse believers from all corners of the Earth, extended religious liberty to them, avoided bloody sectarian conflict, and flourished on the world historical stage, all under the aegis of the oldest still-operative written Constitution in the world.[3] The most remarkable thing about the Founders' theory of religious liberty is that, by world historical standards, the experiment has been a singular success.

The ingredients of this unique achievement are several and varied, but chief among them has to be the political genius of the Founders. The Founders knew that religion could destabilize the republic they established, just as they knew that religion was essential to its success. The Founders knew that the social and political liabilities of religious faith had to be defused (or at least diffused), but they knew also that faith's social and political assets had to be cultivated if the republic was to flourish. As they wrote in the Northwest Ordinance of 1789, religion (along with morality and knowledge) is "essential to good government and the happiness of mankind."

The Founders knew that religious liberty was the fire with which they must play—a dangerous but essential aspect of civil society. Their genius lies, most precisely stated, in this: They devised constitutional doctrines that dissipated the centrifugal force of religion while retaining its centripetal tendencies. They did not secularize the public realm. They did not seek to impose uniformity of religious opinion. Religion was not for the state to coerce, manage, or oversee; it was for

---

2. *School District of Abington Township v. Schempp*, 374 U.S. 203, 213 (1963).

3. National constitution, that is. Some extant state constitutions, such as those in Vermont (1777) and Massachusetts (1780), were written during the Revolution.

churches and for persons, all acting freely and out of conviction. But the state would—because it needed to—promote religion, encourage it, and partner with it, all for the sake of the common good.

Their constitutional settlement has endured for almost two centuries. Succinctly stated, the Founders believed that the federal government's promotion of religion and partnership with religious institutions, without coercion or establishment of any particular sect, is not only constitutionally permissible, but also essential, both to ensure the survival of the republic and for the flourishing of the people who compose it. The formula was freedom within a robustly religious culture, a religious culture cultivated assiduously—though deftly—by the public authority.

The settlement included the political community's affirmation of certain natural truths about God. The divine realities affirmed in the Declaration of Independence—a unitary God Who created all there is, Who providentially guides human events, and Whose effects included naturally known moral truths—could be and were known by reason alone. These truths are elements of a "natural theology" or "natural religion," which is really a branch of philosophy. Promoting respect for and belief in them was part of the common good entrusted to the care of public authority.

The political community's common life did not extend to what distinguished the various churches, one from the others. The Founders' most important insight into religious liberty as a civil right was to see that the truth about sectarian matters—sacred doctrine, modes of worship, forms of church polity, rules for church membership in good standing—could be kept out of political life. Mentally bracketing the truth about such matters did not imply that persons could do as they please so long as they claim a religious basis for their behavior. It meant instead that legal regulation of any acts that allegedly served such religious ends had to be based on other reasons, such as proper care for public peace, safety, or morality.

The First Amendment put the churches on an equal footing: No establishment of religion is constitutionally permissible at the federal level. The Supreme Court repudiated this resilient constitutional design at almost the exact moment the American people had achieved a real and stable pluralism of equal faiths. In the 1962 public-school prayer case, *Engel v. Vitale*,[4] the Court declared that voluntary affirmation of natural religion in the public schools was unconstitutional. (New York's students were led in the daily recitation of "Almighty God we acknowledge our dependence upon thee, and we beg Thy blessings upon us, our parents, our teachers, and our Country.") *Engel* christened a new master norm of constitutional law: Neither the states nor the federal government may promote or foster or aid religion, even if there is no coercion or preference among believers. "Separation of church and state" meant mutual abstention of the two spheres. The state and its sphere were to be wholly secular; religious

---

4.   The Court anticipated the secularism of *Engel* during a brief (1947–1952) earlier experiment with church–state doctrine. First in *dictum* in *Everson v. Board of Education* (330 U.S. 1 (1947)) and then as the holding a year later in *McCollum v. Board of Education* (333 U.S. 203), Court majorities said that the constitutional command of the Founders was a "high wall of separation"—meaning a secularized public square. This experiment was stillborn. The secularist thrust of these cases had little effect on lower courts and almost none upon political figures (save to generate opposition to the Court). The Supreme Court itself abandoned the experiment in 1952 in *Zorach v. Clausen*. See Chapter 5, *infra*. Not until 1961 did the Court signal that its secularist doctrines of the late 1940s were poised for a comeback, a return accomplished in *Engel* (1962). See Chapter 6, *infra*.

life was entirely private. Religion and politics traveled on parallel arcs of mutually exclusive concerns.

With *Engel*, the Supreme Court launched a campaign to privatize religion. This constitutional revolution was not a pogrom, an attempt to stamp out religious belief or to impose (somehow) upon the American body politic a militant atheism. The goal was relocation, not eradication. The Court mandated secularism; that is, the absence of God from law and politics, what Richard John Neuhaus famously calls the "naked public square."[5] Religion was benignly assigned to its natural habitat, the Court repeatedly said: the realm of the individual, the family, the church.

The Court's most common justification for its privatizing campaign was that it is what the Founders commanded. One intended effect of this monograph is to expose the Court's history as fiction. In truth, the *Engel* initiative was the Court's conviction that America would be better if its public life was secularized. There were and are many sources of this conviction. Among them are judicial enchantment with the idea that individual experience, not regimented church life or doctrine and creed, is the real stuff of religion; the perceived implications of "our democratic way of life"; and the belief that privatized religion was a corollary of or a necessary means to achieving racial equality.

The Court's privatizing campaign reached its high-water mark in 1985. The tide has slowly but steadily gone out since. We stand now (to switch the metaphor) at a fork in the road, one path of which runs back to the Founders' vision, a vision that the great majority of Americans continue to share.

---

5. Richard John Neuhaus, *The Naked Public Square: Religion and Democracy in America* (Grand Rapids, Mich.: Wm. B. Eerdman's Publishing, 1986).

This monograph will explain the Founders' theory of religious liberty and how the Supreme Court deviated from the Founders' approach in the 20th century. The first three chapters will describe the Founders' view of the relationship between religion and politics and illustrate this relationship by summoning historical evidence. The remaining chapters will describe the Supreme Court's movement away from the Founders' view, starting in 1947 with the infamous case of *Everson v. Ewing Township Board of Education*, in the context of the social and theological climate that influenced the Court's rulings.

The last two chapters will show how the Court's skewed interpretation of the Religion Clause has led to contradictory outcomes, where the Court has ruled that government is unable to secure free exercise without "establishing" a religion and that the Ten Commandments is both constitutional and unconstitutional. The implication is that the Court's interpretation of the Establishment Clause is wrong as a matter of constitutional interpretation, has resulted in bad policy, and needs to be revisited and revised.

Chapter 1

THE FOUNDERS'
ACHIEVEMENTS

$\mathcal{T}$he "Founding" comprises the years from 1776 to 1791, the time between the first volleys of revolution at Lexington and ratification of the Bill of Rights. The Founding began when our forefathers threw off one political identity (that of British colonials) and cemented another: citizens of the United States of America. The Founding thus embraces the Revolutionary War, the failed Articles of Confederation, the 1787 Philadelphia constitutional convention, and the subsequent ratification struggle. During that contest, Madison, Alexander Hamilton, and John Jay published *The Federalist Papers*. The Founding also includes the beginnings of our national government—Washington's inauguration, all the meetings of the First Congress, the establishment of Cabinet departments, and the states' approval of the Bill of Rights.

While religious conflict was not at the heart of the colonies' break with Great Britain or central to the failures of the Articles of Confederation, we cannot understand the Founding or the people whose founding it was without understanding their religion. The American people were a God-fearing Christian and largely Protestant people. Some among them were skeptical of revelation; a few, Thomas Jefferson included, denied the possibility of revelation (though not the existence of God). The vast majority of the Founders were not, in any event, Jeffersonians in faith.

Historians disagree about how "churched" the American people were near the end of the 18th century. Studies indicate that rates of church membership and attendance were not as high then as during the "Second Great Awakening" of the 1840s or during the 1950s. But being "churched" is one way of being religious. Many leading figures in American history—from Jefferson to Abraham Lincoln to Ronald Reagan—have been religious but not churched. Even non-religious people may inhabit a culture in which the common stock of concepts, language, beliefs—in sum, the worldview on offer—is religious. In fact, the Founding occurred within a religious culture inhabited by religious people. Atheism was not then a culturally sustainable option. A "naked public square" was scarcely imaginable.

In this chapter, we shall explore five characteristics of the Founders' church–state settlement, its contours and presuppositions. We shall explore them partly by contrasting them to the modern Supreme Court's novel reinterpretations of them.

RELIGIOUS TRUTH AND PUBLIC LIFE

Confidence in human reason was characteristic of the founding generation. To modern ears this might sound like saying that the Founders were skeptical of religion or that they were rationalists; that is, unbelievers. Not so. At the time of the Founding, any reasonable person was expected to affirm the truths of the Declaration of Independence—there was a divine Creator Who providently guided human affairs, chiefly through provision of moral truths such as those concerning human inalienable rights—and most did. The Founders appealed to the "Laws of Nature and of Nature's God." Their point was that there is a higher moral law—and a Supreme Lawgiver—to which even the monarch of the world's most powerful country should submit. Just in case the earthly king demurred, God's creatures could appeal to transcendent morality to justify a revolt. Call these propositions the elements of "natural religion," and contrast them with the tenets of "positive theology" or revealed truth.

Where public authority and ordinary citizens *qua* citizens affirm that there is a God—as they do in the National Motto or the Pledge of Allegiance and as Lincoln did in his Second Inaugural—they do not abandon what would today be called secular purposes for lawmaking. "Secular" is a term deployed much later in our constitutional tradition; the Founders did not use it when they talked about religion and the polity. For them the commonweal included care for religion, even as the distinctive beliefs and practices of the sects were (in effect) deemed to be beyond the ken of public authority so long as the actions of believers are in accord with general laws. Promoting religion was a proper governmental action because affirming the existence of God and supporting religion promotes the common good.

There was an end to it: Trying to decide whether doing those things was "secular" or "religious" (or, I suppose, "sectarian") was not important. "Good government" and "the happiness of humankind" required it. Where government promoted natural religion, and where it cooperated with the churches in education and welfare projects for the common good, it did not affirm any sect's distinctive message or practices; it merely recognized that religious institutions played a role in promoting the common good.

Where matters of theology and revelation and doctrine are instead described as irrational, or as ineffable raw experience, or as subjective projections, belief is undermined. One venturing into the realm of the sects then leaves behind both reason and any connection to the rules of inquiry and debate about public matters. This has unfortunately been the dominant message about religion on offer from the Supreme Court since the early 1960s. (See below, "The Equality of Religious Sects," in this chapter.)

RELIGIOUS TRUTH AND RELIGIOUS LIBERTY

Our tradition of religious liberty is founded in convictions such as those expressed by James Madison, our fourth President and a moving force behind the enactment of our Bill of Rights. In his 1786 *Memorial and Remonstrance*, Madison argued that "religion or the duty which we owe to our Creator and the Manner of discharging it, can be directed only by reason and conviction, not by force or violence." Madison did not affirm these sentiments as a hypothesis. He affirmed them as true.

Religious liberty for the Founders was basically what it is for most believers (but not for most elites) today: a matter of discerning the truth about God, adhering to it once discerned, and then doing one's duty as prescribed by God within the confines of generally applicable laws that secure the safety and happiness of the community. The Founders were accurately described by the Supreme Court in 1963—albeit, by then, a Court with a decidedly different worldview—as "believ[ing] devotedly that there was a God and that the unalienable rights of Men were rooted in Him."[6] Religious liberty was the central "unalienable right."

For today's Court, however, "religious liberty" is something very different. It is species of a genus, and an inferior or mutilated kind of species at that. The Court understands liberty to mean personal autonomy and self-definition. Said by

---

6.   *School District of Abington Township v. Schempp*, 374 U.S. 203 (1963), 213.

the Court to be the "heart of liberty," this means, the Court stipulated in 1992, the "right to define one's own concept of existence, of meaning, the universe, and of the mystery of human life."[7] In this construal of "liberty," one's beliefs are genuine and authentic—and thus make you who you really are—by virtue of your holding them as distinctly yours. The great sociologist of religion Thomas Luckmann refers to this phenomenon as "something like a sacred status" that the "dominant themes in the modern sacred cosmos bestow...upon the individual himself by articulating his autonomy."[8]

The difference is that most believers today do not hold their beliefs in order to make a statement about their individuality. The believer holds his beliefs not as "one's own," but as the way things truly and objectively are. Believers characteristically profess adherence to truths revealed, taught, preached by someone else—the prophet or the rabbi, for instance. Believers usually seek to hold whatever it is that others do *not* hold. Believers typically worship in community, where they believe what others believe and rejoice in their common belief. Believers see themselves as followers, disciples, adherents, even as humble sinners who stand under divine judgment.

Within the Court's new worldview, however, most religious believers occupy an inferior status. They cling to the deliverances of someone else. They are both victims and perpetrators of dreaded heteronomy. Theirs is a servile life; their "liberty" is and can only be tolerated as second-best, unwise, largely a waste because it makes a person hollow and inauthentic.

---

7. *Planned Parenthood of Southeastern Pennsylvania v. Casey*, 505 U.S. 833 (1992).

8. Thomas Luckmann, "Shrinking Transcendence, Expanding Religion?" 51 *Sociological Analysis*, No. 2 (Summer 1990), 138.

RELIGION'S POLITICAL DIVISIVENESS

The Supreme Court since 1962 has worried about religion's political divisiveness. The justices regularly express terrible fears for the republic's safety should their privatization campaign falter. These justices have never related their fears, however, to their own reinvention of religious liberty. Given the solipsism and narcissism at the "heart" of their idea of "liberty," one wonders how genuine political fraternity rooted in an objective common good could be possible. The justices instead trace their fear of sectarian conflict to the Founders and the incendiary potential for conflict to traditional religion itself. Most important, the Court has invariably attributed to the Founders the solution enforced by the modern Court; namely, that of private religion and the secular public square. It is a garbled historical translation at the very best.

The Founders stood too close in time to wars of religion in their British homeland to overlook religion's potential divisiveness. They had recently come through an armed conflict with the French and Indians for control of North America, a conflict suffused with age-old animosity between Catholic France and Protestant England. Few of those who assembled in Philadelphia to draft the Declaration of Independence and, later, to write the Constitution were themselves born abroad, but they were all descendants of immigrants who, in many cases, fled to America in search of religious freedom. Though we look upon the Founders' society as remarkably homogeneous, they considered it to be religiously diverse and perilously inclined to sectarian conflict. The Founders possessed no confidence born of successful social experiments with religious liberty in diverse societies. They could not have—because there were none.

The Supreme Court began saying shortly after World War II that political division along religious lines was the paramount concern of the Founders, to which the First Amendment was the solution. This is untrue. We have already seen (and later will explore further) that the Founders were more concerned to vouchsafe to persons the freedom to do what God required of them. On the social effects of religion, the Founders were more concerned to preserve the political benefits of a religious populace than they were to combat its evil side effects. The Founders nonetheless worried about religion's "divisiveness," and the First Amendment was indeed their solution to it.

Those who founded our nation by establishing the Constitution as supreme law of the land surely sought political peace. Theirs would have been a curious "founding" indeed had they not done so. They feared the potential mischief of religious factions and were wary of the political mastery of religion more generally. But a wholly private religion and a secularized public space were, insofar as these realities were intelligible to them, false and politically suicidal.

The Founders were acutely aware of the problem (as they called it) of "faction"—what we would more likely call "special interests" (save that for Madison, a "faction" could constitute a numerical majority of voters so long as they were acting contrary to the true public good). Madison's *Federalist* No. 10 examined the generic problem of which sectarian political activity was one species. Madison treated religio-political conflict as one kind of factional discord, among other kinds. "[Z]eal for different opinions concerning religion, concerning government and many other points" "divide[d] mankind into parties, or factions," and the competition among them is often "inflamed." But, Madison concluded, "the most common and durable source of factions has been the various and unequal distribution of property."[9]

Madison's remedy for factions of all types was basically the same: Welcome a multiplication of factions, "extend the sphere" of conflict among them, and hope that a multitude of diverse factions would forestall the achievement of any one's worst designs. "A religious sect may degenerate into a political faction in a part of the Confederacy; but the variety of sects dispersed over the entire face of it must secure the national councils against any danger from that source."[10]

The tonic of *Federalist* No. 10—the multiplicity of interests and sects—was reiterated by Federalists in the ratifying conventions, in the newspapers, and wherever religious liberty was thought to be endangered by the new Constitution. Madison made precisely this argument to the Virginia Convention that ratified the Constitution. Edmund Randolph followed him, speaking to the same effect. Future Supreme Court Justice James Iredell made potent use of it in North Carolina, as did that state's governor, Samuel Johnston. In fact, this argument—that theologico-political contention is inevitable and its effects acceptable in an extended republic—was made wherever the "Publius" series circulated. There was nothing of the "naked public square" in it.

"Divisiveness" due to religion is surely part of the Founders' story about church and state. Not only did they soberly judge, however, that the political system *could* handle that sort of conflict; they constructed and justified our constitutional order, in part, specifically *to* handle it. Madison argued in *Federalist* No. 10 that the "latent causes of faction," including religious causes, are "sown in the nature of man" and cannot be eradicated.[11]

---

9. *The Federalist* No. 10, George W. Carey and James McClellan, eds. (Indianapolis, Ind.: Liberty Fund, Inc.), 44.

10. *Ibid.*, 48.

11. *Ibid.*, 43.

It is, finally, curious that the Supreme Court fell under the spell of "divisiveness" precisely at a time—the late 1960s through the 1970s—when America's religious groups were more tolerant of each other than ever before. It is also curious that the Court declared to take no risks associated with the public religion precisely when, in other areas of constitutional law like race, sexual matters, and criminal procedure, the justices took the position that no amount of social turmoil would deter the Court from doing the right thing.

THE EQUALITY OF RELIGIOUS SECTS

The Founders engineered their constitutional plan for church and state around the term *sect*. Views on such distinctly religious matters as the content of creeds and books of doctrine; liturgy or modes of worship; styles of church governance (hierarchical or congregational, national or local or regional); and internal church discipline (what qualifies or disqualifies an adherent for community membership) were all—in the law's eyes—to be treated as neither true nor false.

Doctrine, discipline, worship, governance were within the province of faith, characteristic of the sects. Contending accounts of these matters were matters of opinion. Heresy and dogma were theological concepts. They were not legally cognizable. The doctrines of (for example) Presbyterians, Catholics, and Jews were neither "dogma" nor "heresy"—even if adherents of those faiths said so (of the others) and even if (because some of the doctrines were incompatible) one or more of them actually had to be false. Government's purpose was to protect the right to practice one's faith as long as doing so did not violate the rights of others or the requirements of the common good.

The Founders stipulated a sort of mental discipline for lawmakers. The First Amendment obliged those exercising public authority to refrain from making the truth or falsity of theological propositions a basis for legislation. This could be difficult for members of the founding generation. By and large they held that such matters were propositions: assertions that could be either true or false. The First Amendment meant that the truth or falsity of such matters had to be put aside in civil affairs. The First Amendment neither stipulated not supposed that the truth or falsity of these things did not exist; it said that the validity of these propositions was beyond the competence of public authority.

Had the Founders thought more like some of today's elites, they could have complied effortlessly with the First Amendment. One who is obliged by law to refrain from making, say, the truth about the most beautiful color a reason for public action has no trouble doing so. There is no truth about the most beautiful color; it is all a matter of opinion. For that reason, the public servant naturally and easily puts the "truth" about color aside in handling affairs of state.

The Supreme Court has lately treated religion as if it were about colors. People have their favorite colors, a choice that many of them defend by appeal to the "truth" about which color is best, but one's favorite color is a fact about one's preferences and no more than that. That is how the Court has treated religion for several decades: a personal predilection with no higher cognitive ground than one's adherence to blue, to Starbucks, or to the Chicago Bears. People sometimes get excited about which color or coffee or sports team is best. Some dispute the matter vigorously. But fighting over these differences makes as much sense as fighting over the differences between Oreos and Chips Ahoy cookies.

As early as 1944, in *Ballard v. United States*, Justice Robert Jackson wrote of religion that such "experiences, like some tones and colors, have existence for one, but not at all for another."[12] A few years later, Justice Stanley Reed wrote for the Court that "what is one man's amusement, teaches another's doctrine."[13]

We see, too, at about this time the Court's first flirtation with the secularized public sphere. Did the Court first imagine that religion was entirely subjective and then go on to see that it could not contribute in any positive way to law and politics? Or did the Court first imagine a secularized public realm—perhaps one, managed according to progressive principles of scientific public administration, from which the plague of authoritarian religion had been banished—and then rationalize the choice by discrediting religion? Or was it a dialectical movement between the two? It may be impossible to provide a definitive answer.

THE HISTORICAL "COMMAND" OF THE FOUNDERS

The struggle to ratify the proposed Constitution was the birthplace of the First Amendment Religion Clauses. Advocates of the Constitution (Federalists) were obliged by their opponents' (Anti-Federalists) criticisms to work for amendments in the form of a bill of rights.

Which rights (in general) did the Anti-Federalists wish to preserve more explicitly against possible federal encroachment? Virginia's Richard Henry Lee (a little later a member of the

---

[12.] *United States v. Ballard*, 322 U.S. 78, 95 (1944). In this case, the Court ruled that the government cannot require a jury to determine whether a defendant's religious beliefs are true or false. To do so violates the Free Exercise Clause.

[13.] *Winters v. New York*, 333 U.S. 507, 510 (1948). The Court in this case ruled that a New York law banning lurid crime books was overly vague and violated the First Amendment's guarantee of freedom of speech.

first United States Senate) looked to the "various Bills or declarations of Rights whereon the Governments of the greater number of the States are founded."[14] Former Governor and revolutionary firebrand Patrick Henry embraced this option during the Virginia ratification conclave, as did George Mason, who remains the Founder whose influence has been most underappreciated by subsequent historians. They all wanted protections like those that were found in the Virginia Declaration of Rights. Anti-Federalist concern in North Carolina focused on losing rights secured under the North Carolina Constitution. In the words of many Anti-Federalists, it was precisely because the national government overrode the state constitutions—one Anti-Federalist said the Supremacy Clause was the entire problem—that they feared for their liberties.[15]

What were the Anti-Federalist concerns specific to religion? The basic fear was sect domination leading to the establishment of a national religion. The Pennsylvania Anti-Federalist minority captured the sentiment of the entire movement: "The rights of conscience shall be held inviolable, and neither the legislature, executive nor judicial powers of the United States shall have authority to alter, abrogate or infringe any part of the constitutions of the several states, which provide for the preservation of liberty in matters of religion."[16] One North Carolina delegate inquired whether a national establishment would be Episcopal or Presbyterian.[17] William Spaight, a drafter of the Constitution and later a Senator from

---

14. J. Ballagh, 2 *Letters of Richard Henry Lee* 442–43 (1911).

15. See G. Bradley, *Church–State Relationships in America* (Greenwood Press, 1987), 79.

16. B. McMaster and F. Stone, eds., *Pennsylvania and the Federal Constitution 1787–1788*, 421 (1970).

17. 4 *Eliot's Debates* at 191–192.

North Carolina, urged that "no sect be preferred to another."[18]

Madison argued that "no one sect will ever be able to out-number or depress the rest."[19] North Carolina Governor Sam-uel Johnston insisted that there was no basis to fear "that any one religious sect shall be exclusively established": Indeed, he knew "but two or three states where there is the least chance of establishing any particular religion," noting Massachusetts and Connecticut.[20] Edmund Randolph assured Virginia's Anti-Federalists that the variety of beliefs "will prevent the estab-lishment of any one sect, in prejudice to the rest."[21] Zachariah Johnson similarly counseled that "the difficulty of establishing a uniformity of religion in this country is immense."[22] Still, the fear of sect-preference persisted.

Madison was the House floor manager for the amend-ments that became our Bill of Rights. This role, along with his contributions to the Virginia struggle over tax assessment to support teachers of religion as well as his later service as Presi-dent, makes him the most authoritative on the original mean-ing of the Religion Clause. All too often, however, recent court decisions have wondered about Madison's philosophy or the-ory of church–state relations and ignored what the Religious Clauses meant.

A notable exception to this misplaced focus is Justice Wil-liam Rehnquist, later the Chief Justice of the United States. In his dissenting opinion in *Wallace v. Jaffree*, the 1985 case invali-dating a public school "moment-of-silence" law, Rehnquist wrote that Madison's "sponsorship of the Amendments was

---

18. *Ibid.* at 208.
19. 3 *Eliot's* at 330.
20. 4 *Eliot's* at 199.
21. 3 *Eliot's* at 204.
22. *Ibid.* at 645.

obviously not that of a zealous believer in the necessity of the Religion Clauses, but of one who felt that it might do some good, could do no harm, and would satisfy those who had ratified the Constitution on the condition that Congress propose a Bill of Rights."[23] Just so: Madison said of his proposed Bill of Rights that its provisions "are restrained to points on which least difficulty was apprehended.... Nothing of a controvertible nature ought to be hazarded by those who are sincere in wishing for the approbation of each House, and of the State Legislatures." As if to justify himself to Jefferson, he wrote that "every thing of a controvertible nature" was "studiously avoided."[24]

When we look at what Madison did and said to gain passage of the Religion Clause, we see the following. Madison's initial House proposal was proffered on June 8, 1789. It was cobbled together from the work of the various state conventions: "The civil rights of none shall be abridged on account of religious belief or worship, *nor shall any national religion be established*, nor shall the full and equal rights of conscience be in any manner, or on any pretext, infringed."[25]

Madison expressly defined on the House floor what he meant by the emphasized provision. He said that it responded to the fear that "one sect might obtain a pre-eminence, or two combine together, and establish a religion to which they would compel others to conform."[26] When the wording was pared down to "no religion shall be established by law, nor shall the equal rights of conscience be infringed," Madison again provided a public interpretation. He "apprehended the

---

23. 472 U.S. at 98.
24. 12 *Papers of James Madison*, 272 (Robert A. Ruttland & Charles F. Hobson, eds. 1977).
25. 1 Annals of Congress 434. Emphasis added.
26. *Ibid.* at 731.

meaning of the words to be, that Congress should not establish a religion, and enforce the legal observation of it by law, nor compel men to worship God in any manner contrary to their conscience."[27] Nowhere in either published or private debate during this period did Madison deviate from these pronouncements.

Rehnquist accurately summarized the whole congressional debate in his *Wallace v. Jaffree* dissent. Speaking with specific reference to the House discussion of August 15, 1789, Rehnquist said that "none" of the discussants that day "expressed the slightest indication that they thought the language before them from the Select Committee, or the evil to be aimed at, would require that the Government be absolutely neutral as between religion and irreligion." He quite rightly observed also that the debates reveal that the evil to be forestalled was "the establishment of a national church, and perhaps the preference of one religious sect over another; but it was definitely not concerned about whether the Government might aid all religions evenhandedly."

---

27. *Ibid.* at 729.

Chapter 2

RELIGION AND MORALITY: ANCHORS OF REPUBLICAN GOVERNMENT

"Your Constitution is all sail and no anchor," Lord Thomas Macaulay famously wrote to Jefferson's first scholarly biographer, Henry Randall.[28] Macaulay was no fan of Jefferson, largely because Jefferson was a democrat and Macaulay was not. Macaulay thought that giving the masses controlling power over government (as he thought Jefferson would) was to empower a hungry rabble. Is it possible, Macaulay asked Randall in 1857, to doubt what sort of legislator a "distressed majority" will choose?

> On one side is a statesman teaching patience, respect for vested rights, strict observance of public faith. On the other is a demagogue ranting about the tyranny of capitalists and usurists, and asking why anybody should be permitted to drink champagne and to ride in a carriage, while thousands of honest folks are in want of necessaries?[29]

---

28. Thomas B. Macaulay, Letter to Henry S. Randall, May 23, 1857.

Good question. Macaulay did not doubt what a "working-man who hears his children cry for more bread" would do. Nor did he doubt the calamitous effects of his doing so. Democracy "must, sooner or later, destroy liberty or civilization, or both."[30] Not even our heralded Constitution could arrest the descent into anarchy. It was, according to Macaulay, all canvas and no ballast. There was no residuum of power in those who knew better: aristocracy, the propertied, and the civilized. Macaulay thought that Jefferson was an inveterate democrat who was dangerously ignorant of these perils.

The Founders' experiment in liberty was not, as a matter of fact, "all sail and no anchor," although it is easy to see how Macaulay got it wrong. The United States Constitution is almost entirely about government superstructure. It scarcely refers to cultural infrastructure (that is, civil society). But appearances are deceiving. In two distinct but complementary ways, the Constitution provides for ballast enough—though not for the aristocratic sort favored by Macaulay.

First, the Constitution obviously establishes a federal system in which the national government has limited, enumerated powers. This federal power lacks plenary government authority. That is the reserve of the states. The state constitutions set up governments with authority to legislate on family structure, religion, education, public morals—all the glue that holds civil society together. Here are governments fully in charge of an anchor: state authorities that the national Constitution presupposes, depends upon, and protects in many ways (including the guarantee to each of a "republican form of government") and without which there could be no national government. After all, without the states

---

29. *Ibid.*
30. *Ibid.*

there could be no Senators, no Electoral College, no election of House Members.

The other source of Macaulay's mistake is what I call the "missing *Federalist Paper*." Those who drafted the national Constitution worried openly about the "anchor" of democracy: What would give a democratic society the stability it needs to avoid running off course, so to speak, and trampling on the rights of its own citizens? The Founders asked the question explicitly: Is there sufficient virtue among men for self-government? Or, as Madison asked in *Federalist* No. 55, are "nothing less than the chains of despotism" required to "restrain [men] from destroying and devouring one another"?[31]

Madison replied that "republican government presupposes the existence of [virtuous] qualities" in men "in a higher degree than any other form" of government.[32] How would these more "esteem[ed]" qualities be cultivated in the citizenry? The answer lay with the institutions of civil society, especially with the institutions of religion—the churches. The Founders firmly believed that religion was part of the citizenry's republican equipment. Religion had to be free because true belief can come only from within, from one's conscience, as opposed to external coercion by the government. Religion had to be free too, because the alternatives were politically oppressive. But above all else, religion had to be present, or the experiment in liberty would fail.

This is the decisive reason why, unlike the modern Court, the Founders accepted the risks of public religion: They needed it. "Of all the dispositions and habits which lead to political prosperity, Religion and Morality are indispensable supports," Washington said in his Farewell Address.

---

31. *The Federalist* No. 55, Carey ed., 291.
32. *Ibid.*

And let us with caution indulge the supposition, that morality can be maintained without Religion. Whatever may be conceded of the influence of refined education on minds of peculiar structure; reason and experience both forbid us to expect that national morality can prevail in exclusion of religious principle.[33]

John Adams thought that "religion and virtue" were the only foundations not only of republicanism, "but of social felicity under all governments and in all the combinations of human society."[34] Even extreme Baptist hostility to New England orthodoxy did not deviate from Washington's admonition. Reverend Phillips Payson, an influential member of the Protestant clergy during the founding period, opined that:

> [Religion] keeps alive the best sense of moral obligation.... The fear and reverence of God and the terrors of eternity are the most powerful restraints upon the mind of men. And hence it is of special importance in a free government, the spirit of which being always friendly to the sacred rights of conscience, it will hold up the Gospel as the great rule of faith and practice.[35]

Thomas Jefferson is rightly regarded as among the most latitudinarian of the Founders in matters of religion. To him

---

33. George Washington, Farewell Address, September 19, 1796, in Matthew Spalding, ed., *The Founders' Almanac: A Practical Guide to the Notable Events, Greatest Leaders & Most Eloquent Words of the American Founding* (Washington, D.C.: The Heritage Foundation, 2002), 311.

34. John Adams, letter to Benjamin Rush, August 28, 1811.

35. Payson's Election Sermon, 1778, in *The Pulpit of the American Revolution*, with a historical introductions, notes, and illustrations, by John Wingate Thornton, 2d ed. (Boston: D. Lothrop & Co., 1876), 339.

Christianity was both the most sublime and the most perverse system known to the world. But he also subscribed to the "missing *Federalist Paper*" (the need for morality in a republic and the need to promote religion as the "guardian of morals"). Jefferson said in 1781 that liberty in America depended on a popular perception that it was the gift of God, and he thought it politically beneficial if Americans privately decided that there was "only one God, and he all perfect" and that there was a future state of rewards and punishments.[36]

At about the same time, Jefferson drafted a bill for the Virginia Assembly authorizing punishment of ministers who failed to preach sermons at the legislators' command. Jefferson's proposal was a heavy-handed and regrettable application of the Founders' general concern to establish a working partnership between church and state for the common good. Later, President Jefferson negotiated a treaty with the Kaskaskia Indians whose terms included government provision of Catholic missionaries to the tribe, which reveals his understanding that the Constitution does not forbid church and state from partnering in order to achieve the common good.[37]

This type of prominent testimony—what some would call anecdotal evidence—could be multiplied many times over. Let us look now instead at a broader demographic measure of the probative force of these "anecdotes": the Northwest Ordinance of 1787. This act of the Confederation-era Congress extended to the territories the "fundamental principles of civil and religious liberty" guaranteed by the state constitutions. When the Constitution was ratified and the United States government set up in 1789, the first Congress enacted the same law to govern the territories of the new nation.

---

[36]. See Thomas Jefferson, *Notes on the State of Virginia*, Query 18.
[37]. See Bradley, *Church–State Relationships in America*, 100–101.

After ratification of the Bill of Rights, Congress endorsed the 1787 action in its entirety. During the incumbencies of Adams and Jefferson, the Indiana (1800), Michigan (1805), and Illinois (1809) territories were organized by re-enactment of the Northwest Ordinance. President Madison signed the bill organizing the Missouri territory on basically the same footing.

Considered an organic law of the United States, the Northwest Ordinance says, "Religion, morality, and knowledge, being necessary to good government and the happiness of mankind, schools and the means of education shall forever be encouraged." Each of the first four Presidents and a majority of the first 10 Congresses supported this basic law for the territories, a law that harmonized religious liberty with the necessity of promoting religion and morality. These lawmakers, almost to the last man, were drawn from the Founders; that is, from the generation of politically active Americans who broke from England and brought this country into being by ratifying the Constitution and, two years later, the First Amendment. Jefferson and Madison were among them. And they all viewed government aid, encouragement, and support of religion as not only consistent with, but also a part of religious liberty.

To put the Founders' arrangement into philosophical language, religion was part of the common good of their political society. It was not entirely private; it was partly and in a crucial way public too. It surely need not be either/or. Like marriage and family life, religion occupied space in both the public and private spheres. Wise lawmakers understood that religion and family were pre-political goods that people enjoyed before there was an organized government. Civil law supervened upon moral realities, such as religion and family, and regulated them for the benefit of "good government" and the "happiness of humankind."

The Founders held that reason could lead a person to affirm "natural religion," and most men did affirm it. They also affirmed that public religion was a common benefit. Everyone in society enjoyed the benefits of religion, even those who were not personally devout. Just as everyone in our society benefits by having an educated citizenry, the Founders knew that even vicious people benefit from a virtuous citizenry, and religion was essential to virtue. Therefore, everyone in society benefits from public support of religions that teach citizens to respect the rights of others and behave in a virtuous manner, even those who do not adhere to the specific tenets of the supported religion.

Let us now take a closer look at just what those who supported the Northwest Ordinance affirmed: "Religion, morality, and knowledge, being necessary to good government and the happiness of humankind. . . ." That is to say that religion, morality, and knowledge *are* necessary. But how so? Some people at the Founding thought that one needed religion to know the good; others, that one needed it to *be* good.

The first group believed that the intellect and character of humans were so corrupted by sin that good and evil appeared to them as gauzy, indistinct alternatives, all the more evanescent because humans were prone to rationalize their sinful ways. What we see in our rearview mirrors we easily convince ourselves is fine, or as good as it can be in this world. Religion drops the scales from our eyes. It is worth noting here that even those relatively few Founders whose confidence in revelation wavered never lost belief in objective morality. Insofar as they perceived that the gradual loss of faith in revealed truth might endanger belief in the norms of the Decalogue, they earnestly sought more secure ground for those norms by separating them from revealed truth. Jefferson was one such person.

Other people at the Founding thought that the human mind, despite the corrupting effects of Adam's and Eve's fall from grace, could grasp the truths of morality. Some behavior was known by and through reason to be wrong for everybody, in all places and at all times. These acts were not wrong because humans had decided to call them wrong or because some king or legislature said they were wrong. They were naturally wrong. The second group realized, however, that we all needed help to be good. Religion was the greatest of all helps because it promised eternal reward to the righteous and misery forever to the evil.

The two groups together constituted more than a consensus of the founding generation. They *were* the founding generation. The affirmations of the Northwest Ordinance represent the all but universal convictions of Americans well into the 19th century and a consensus for some time thereafter.

THE FOUNDERS IN ACTION: PUBLIC SUPPORT FOR RELIGION

The territorial regime established during the Confederation, expressly validated and continued by the First Congress and its successors, was suffused with aid, encouragement, and support for religion. The territories, governed ultimately by Congress, immediately by its appointees, and subject to the limits of the Establishment Clause, were patrons of publicly supported religion *and* religious liberty. The 1787 ordinance expressly repealed a temporary measure for territorial governance passed on April 23, 1784, and became the constitution, or organic law, of the territories until statehood was attained. The land so organized was still largely unsettled, but the method of ongoing land distribution was set in 1785.

Much of the Ohio territory was sold by the Confederation in chunks of several million acres to speculators for resale to individual buyers. In July 1787, the Confederation Congress stipulated in a contract of sale to the Ohio Company that "lot No. 16" in each township be reserved for schools and that "lot No. 29" "be given perpetually for the purposes of religion." Additionally, two complete townships were held "for purposes of a university."[38] These recommendations, drafted by a committee of four, which included Madison, were also incorporated in another large purchase by a consortium headed by John Symmes. Prior to reorganization under the Confederation, Ohio residents were subject to parish taxes, as were residents of the states—chiefly Connecticut—claiming the territory.

Voting for these sale provisions were men who would serve in the First Congress under the Constitution, such as Senators Lee and Grayson of Virginia, William Few of Georgia, Congressman James Schureman of New Jersey, and Congressman Daniel Huger of South Carolina. Grayson explained the reservation's rationale in a letter to George Washington: "The [public support of religion and education] idea holds forth an inducement for neighborhoods of the same religious sentiments to confederate for the purpose of purchasing and settling together."[39]

Illinois residents came into their publicly supported churches through a different route, although also via the offices of James Madison. In September 1788, just after the Virginia ratifying convention, Madison headed a committee of three that rectified an "omission" in previous acts governing "Illinois and Post St. Vincennes." Omitted were "grants of

---

38. See Charles M. Walker, *History of Athens County, Ohio* (Cincinnati: Robert Clarke & Co., 1869), 552.
39. 8 *Letters of George Washington* at 95.

land for Supporting Religion and for Schools" as had been done in western land sales. A tract of land adjoining each village "was reserved forever" for the "sole and only use of supporting the ministry of Religion in such Village." Another tract was designated for schools.[40]

All these reservations of land for religious purposes might suggest the appearance of an establishment, even of sect-preference, but the Founders did not consider public support for religion—just as such—to be an "establishment." They did consider government partiality toward a particular church to be an "establishment." But the Founders—and many succeeding generations of Americans—recognized that any particular, finite task for which the state sought a religious partner could not be performed by *all* the churches, or all the churches would apply to perform it. Besides, there was just so much land available in a township for charitable and religious purposes.

In these circumstances, the results of government distribution could not be "sect-neutral"; one church or another would naturally predominate in the performance of certain tasks or emerge as the preponderant beneficiary of government aid: Even today, Catholic schools are "overrepresented" among beneficiaries of any public aid to religious schools, as the Evangelical "Prison Fellowship" seems to be in serving inmates. The critical thing as far as the Constitution goes is that the distribution pattern—whatever it is—not be influenced by government siding with the theological tenets of any church or with a sect's distinctive mode of worship or internal discipline.

Land distribution policy converged with another strand of territorial administration in grants to missionary societies to

---

40. *34 Journal* at 540–542.

underwrite conversion of the frontier Indians. Paying missionaries, which by 1803 included Catholic priests, to "propagate the Gospel amongst the heathens" was a continuous feature of federal Indian relations from 1785 until at least 1896, when Congress was appropriating $500,000 annually in support of sectarian missions to the Indians.[41] During the first decade after the Establishment Clause took effect, successive Congresses appropriated approximately 12,000 acres of land for one society, the United Brethren, for its efforts among the Indians in the Northwest Territories.[42]

This policy began with the initial distribution ordinance of May 20, 1785, which reserved three townships for the use of "Christian Indians" formerly settled there.[43] In July 1787, Congress enacted, along with the Northwest Ordinance, a reserve of 10,000 acres adjoining the towns and vested it in the United Brethren for "civilizing the Indians."[44] On September 3, 1787, Madison implemented the arrangement by reporting a recommendation that the geographer survey the designated tracts "as speedily as possible" and convey to the Brethren the "intermediate spaces" at the prevailing rates.[45] While not granting new lands, the Fourth, Fifth, Sixth, and

---

[41.] See Andrew L. Cord, *Separation of Church and State: Historical Fact and Current Fiction* (Carlson, 1982), 38.

[42.] *Ibid.*, 43–44.

[43.] Copy of Act in Payson Treat, *The National Land System 1785–1820*, *Appendix II* (1910): "And be it further ordained, that the towns of Grandenhutten, Schoenbrunn, and Salem, on the Muskingum, and so much of the lands adjoining to the said towns, with the buildings and improvements thereon, shall be reserved for the sole use of the Christian Indians, who formerly settled there, or the remains of that society, as may, in the judgment of the geographer, be sufficient for them to cultivate."

[44.] 33 *Journal* at 429–430.

[45.] 34 *Journal* at 485–487.

Seventh Congresses all endorsed this arrangement with the United Brethren.[46]

The most interesting instance of treaty obligations regarding sectarian missions occurred in 1803 when President Jefferson asked the Senate to ratify a treaty with the Kaskaskia Indians. The treaty required the United States to pay a Catholic priest $100 annually for ministration to the tribe.[47] The document, which the Senate ratified, also appropriated $300 for erection of a Catholic church.[48] Jefferson was hardly unique among Presidents in employing religion for public purposes, especially among the Indians, but if even he did not find such acts to be unconstitutional, who among the founding generation could have believed the Establishment Clause forbade aid to religion?

Orleans territory, which constituted the present state of Louisiana, is the most revealing instance. Specifically enjoined to respect the Constitution by President Jefferson and the Eighth Congress, the territorial legislature promptly proceeded to sponsor religious institutions. The territorial university was founded in 1805 on the cornerstone of "learning," "the ablest advocate of genuine liberty and the best supporter of rational religion."[49] Nor did President Jefferson or Secretary of State Madison protest when all religious property was exempted from taxation[50] and when Sabbath observance was enjoined,[51] not to coerce belief but to promote the undisturbed enjoyment of the Sabbath for those who held themselves religiously obliged. Neither Jefferson nor Madison

---

46. Cord, *Separation*, 44.

47. *Ibid.*, 38.

48. *Ibid.*

49. *States of Orleans Territory*, ch. 30, April 19, 1805.

50. *Ibid.* at ch. 31, June 7, 1806.

51. *Ibid.* at ch. 33, June 7, 1806.

objected when (as was common in Virginia) church construction was underwritten by a legislative exception to the ban on lotteries,[52] or when the legislature appointed the governor and the "person exercising the function of chief of the Catholic church" in the territory as superintendents of New Orleans' charity hospital.[53]

President Madison lodged no objection to these practices in accepting Louisiana State into the Union or in subsequently setting up Missouri territory (formerly Louisiana territory) on the same footing as Orleans.[54]

The Founders believed that the religious habits and beliefs of the citizens were Macaulay's "anchor." In terms perhaps familiar to our ears but not to theirs, one could say that the Founders recognized that socialization was essential to people's happiness and to the success of their republican governments. But a republic committed to religious liberty was restricted in its choice of means for bringing about the necessary level of religiosity. The solution—perhaps the only one available—was to authorize government to promote and to partner with religious institutions of civil society. As we have seen in the preceding pages, there is abundant evidence that this is exactly what the founding generation did.

---

52. *Ibid.* at ch. 19, March 6, 1810.
53. *Ibid.* at ch. 6, March 8, 1808.
54. *2 U.S. Statutes at Large* 743 (1812).

Chapter 3

THE STABILITY
OF THE FOUNDERS'
CONSTITUTIONAL DESIGN

*T*he hardiness of the Founders' constitutional doctrines and the resiliency of their presuppositions about faith, character, and liberty do not mean that American religion has been locked in a time warp since 1787. Far from it: The household of American faith has experienced enormous and unanticipated changes running alongside surprising continuities. Americans remain remarkably God-fearing, registering levels of belief and commitment to Christianity comparable to those of the Founding. On the other hand, the Founders could scarcely have anticipated that the two leading Christian denominations in America would be Roman Catholic and Baptist.

Beneath the enduring constitutional settlement lay important changes in the landscape of American faith, especially in American Protestantism. The nature of religious belief has changed. Chief among these changes is probably the "romantic" turn in faith, a move to what the great historian of Christian theology Jaroslav Pelikan calls theology of the heart.

The turn inward to one's experience of the divine as the ground of faith gradually transposed Christian doctrine from the category of propositional truths—the Founders' view. It was a move initiated up to a point by the Founding-era Baptists and Methodists, given consummate theological expression by Friedrich Schleiermacher in the early 19th century, and propelled forward by mid–19th century Romanticism. These developments culminated in the Court's reasoning in *Engel v. Vitale* and *U.S. v. Seeger*, discussed at length in Chapter 6.

Moreover, after the Civil War, Reconstruction marked the emergence of what historian James Turner calls a culturally sustainable atheism. "Colonel" Robert Ingersoll then began making money, for example, as a roving novelty act, as a fish out of water. Audiences were often invited to "Hear Ingersoll the Atheist." Ingersoll's notoriety was less significant, however, than the impact of Charles Darwin and Biblical historical criticism. Darwin effectively challenged the veracity of Genesis, at least for those who read that book as a factual description of Creation.[55] The whole Darwinian picture of "progress" through natural selection acting upon random genetic variation also challenged the belief—then as well as now—in divine Providence: Where was the hand of God in a world depicted as a jungle populated by sophisticated apes?

None of these changes within the household of faith implied that constitutional doctrines had to change. In fact, they remained steady until after World War II. The application of settled constitutional norms was affected, however, as new forms of faith emerged on the American scene. Six historical vignettes in this chapter all illustrate the importance of

---

[55] The alternatives to this reading are not, of course, limited to treating Genesis as myth. Another possible reading is allegorical, in which the truths conveyed in that book are taken to be more theological and metaphysical than historical.

understanding how the Founders' principle of religious liberty still applies in contemporary circumstances.

JEFFERSON AND THE DANBURY BAPTISTS

When most people think about what the First Amendment says with regard to religion, they conclude that it builds a "wall of separation" between church and state. In fact, the First Amendment does not say anything about a wall of separation. That phrase comes from a letter that Thomas Jefferson wrote 13 years after the First Amendment was written and ratified by the people.

What did Jefferson actually say and mean? In 1802, replying to an earlier message from the Danbury Baptist Association of Connecticut, Jefferson wrote:

> Believing with you that religion is a matter which lies solely between Man & his God; that he owes account to none other for his faith or his worship; that the legislative powers of the government reach actions only, & not opinions, —I contemplate with sovereign reverence that act of the whole American people which declared that their legislature should "make no law respecting an establishment of religion or prohibiting the free exercise thereof," thus building a wall of separation between Church & State.[56]

[56.] Thomas Jefferson, Letter to Messrs. Nehemiah Dodge, Ephraim Robbins, and Stephen S. Nelson, a committee of the Danbury Baptist association in the state of Connecticut, 1 January 1802, The Papers of Thomas Jefferson (Manuscript Division, Library of Congress), Series I, Box 89, December 2, 1801–January 1, 1802.

In 1876, in *Reynolds v. United States*, the Court followed Jefferson in "summarizing"—the Court's word—the First Amendment by saying that it erected a "wall of separation." But Jefferson used the phrase as simply another way of saying what the First Amendment says ("thus building a wall..."). For neither Jefferson nor the *Reynolds* Court was "wall of separation" meant to say or mean anything other than what is conveyed by the actual terms of the First Amendment. As a "summary," it gets its content from what has already been said.

Let us examine more closely what Jefferson could possibly have meant in this letter by examining Jefferson's other writings and deeds. In his famous *Notes on the State of Virginia*, Jefferson claimed that "it does me no injury for my neighbor to say there are twenty gods, or no god. It neither picks my pocket nor breaks my leg." Many read this passage and wrongly conclude that for Jefferson, government has no legitimate purpose or interest in the religious views of citizens, since its powers "extend to such acts only as are injurious to others." However, Jefferson also asked in the same document: "can the liberties of a nation be thought secure when we have removed their only firm basis, a conviction in the minds of the people that these liberties are the gift of God? That they are not to be violated but with his wrath?"

In other words, Jefferson understood that the only "firm basis" for securing rights and preventing acts that are injurious to others is a firm conviction in the people that God exists and is the source of our rights.

Therefore, when Jefferson writes in his letter to the Danbury Baptists that "the legitimate powers of government reach actions only, & not opinions," he does not mean to say that government cannot support opinions that affect actions. The belief in God supplies the firm basis for ensuring that the actions of citizens are not injurious to others; therefore, Jefferson supported measures to support religious belief as a statesman. For instance, in the 1770s, Jefferson introduced a bill appointing certain days of fasting and thanksgiving. As Governor of Virginia, he issued a proclamation of "solemn thanksgiving and prayer to Almighty God." Even during his presidency, Jefferson attended church services held in Congress, the most public of buildings.

These actions are wholly consistent with his words when one considers Jefferson's statement that men's opinions have a profound influence on their actions and, therefore, that government must be able to support religious beliefs that provide the firm basis for the protection of rights and liberties.

THE MANY WIVES OF MR. REYNOLDS

The *Everson* Court in 1947 summarized its historical findings "[i]n the words of Jefferson[:] the clause against establishment of religion by law was intended to erect 'a wall of separation between church and state'."[57] The Court mined this quotation from *Reynolds v. United States*, and the *Reynolds* Court got it from Jefferson.

Decided in 1878, *Reynolds* was the first of several cases where the Court sustained legislation designed to eliminate Mormon polygamy. The Court held that religious conviction did not privilege polygamy where it was legally forbidden, as it was everywhere in the United States. In the course of its opinion, the Court quoted Jefferson's letter in which he used the phrase "separation of church and state." The Court has since used the phrase and Jefferson's authority behind it several times to buttress its own secularist understanding of the First Amendment.

---

[57]. 330 U.S. at 16.

Reynolds v. United States, 98 U.S. 145 (1878)

Facts of the Case: George Reynolds, a member of the Church of Jesus Christ of Latter-day Saints, married Amelia Jane Shoefield while still married to Mary Ann Tuddenham. As a result, Reynolds was charged with bigamy under §5352 of the Revised Statutes by the District Court for the third judicial district of the Territory of Utah. Reynolds petitioned to the Supreme Court that his conviction should be overturned primarily on the defense that it was his religious duty as a Mormon to practice polygamy.

Decision: In a unanimous decision, the Supreme Court upheld the ruling of the lower court that the principle of free exercise does not warrant violation of general laws that govern actions rather than pure religious beliefs.

Majority Opinion: Writing for the majority, Chief Justice Morrison Waite acknowledged that Congress can pass no law that prohibits the free exercise of religion under the First Amendment. However, the Court relied on Thomas Jefferson's distinction, written in a letter to the Danbury Baptists, between religious beliefs and religious practices: "[T]he legislative powers of the government reach actions only, and not opinions." Chief Justice Waite delivered the majority opinion of the Court, stating that "Laws are made for the government of actions, and while they cannot interfere with mere religious belief and opinions, they may with practices."

Significance: The Court ruled that generally applicable laws that have a secular purpose are not in violation of the Free Exercise Clause of the First Amendment even if they impinge upon religious *practices* that violate such general laws.

The question confronting the *Reynolds* Court was whether the anti-polygamy law violated the First Amendment—and to answer that question they turned to the "times in the midst of which the provision was adopted."[58] In the Founding the justices saw correctly that religious freedom had to do with (the

---

58. *Reynolds v. United States*, 98 U.S. 145, 162 (1878).

Reynolds Court's words) "precepts," "doctrines," "sects" and their "particular" tenets, and protection from law against "failure to attend upon public worship" and for "entertaining heretical opinions."[59] The Court also made reference to Madison's *Memorial and Remonstrance* and, of course, to Jefferson. For these matters of "opinion," Jefferson can now be heard to say to the Danbury Baptists, no man could suffer at the hands of the civil magistrate.

And note well: The *Reynolds* Court never said or implied that Mormon beliefs about polygamy were false. That is, the Court did not attempt to show that Joseph Smith or those following him in religious authority were wrong about what God communicated to him or to them. It was not for the civil law to gauge the correctness or validity of asserted revelations such as those related by Smith and credited by Mr. Reynolds. "Social duties" were other, paramount matters. These "duties" included everyone's obligation to support public morality and the institution of monogamous marriage. One's religious opinion in favor of polygamy did not affect this social duty.

The Church of Jesus Christ of Latter-day Saints abandoned the practice of polygamy in the 1890s under the accumulated pressure by the federal government. What really caused the church to abandon the practice seems to have been the government's threat to strip the church of all its property. Polygamy is still forbidden by the Mormon Church; only a few breakaway sectarians practice it today.

The Court's distinction in *Reynolds* between protected "belief" and unprotected "action" has been a fulcrum of debate over the meaning of the Free Exercise Clause. The debate has been illuminating at times, and we shall look closely at it in Chapter 8, but it is worth remarking now that the

---

59. *Ibid.* at 162–163.

belief-vs.-action distinction unfortunately misses the Founders' mark.

The real basis of free exercise is neither "belief" nor "action." The real distinction has to do with reasons: Congress may pass no law that presupposes the truth or falsity of some asserted revelation of theological speculation. The government may not prohibit plural marriage on the precise ground that the law that has been revealed by God is false. If the government permitted polygamy where it is rooted in cultural traditions or where it was practiced as a form of community care for widows and orphans, then it could not bar polygamy where it was practiced for religious reasons. But the government may prohibit polygamy because respecting monogamy is the social duty of everyone.

CHAPLAINS: CONSTITUTIONAL OR NOT?

On January 21, 1853, the United States Senate Committee on the Judiciary issued its report on "sundry petitions" previously referred to it. These petitions "pray[ed that] Congress abolish the office of Chaplain." The "sundry" petitioners were not identified, but their claim was nonetheless clear and bold: The extant legal provisions for chaplains in the Army and Navy as well as in the two houses of Congress all violated the First Amendment.

In order to decide upon the correctness of the petitioners' claim, the Committee asked reasonably enough: "what is meant by th[e] expression" "an establishment of religion"? "[W]ithout doubt," the Senators answered, it referred to "establishment" in the "mother country, and its meaning is to be ascertained by ascertaining what that establishment was." What was the material meaning? "[T]he *union of church and state* of which our ancestors were so justly jealous" (emphasis added). And that "connection" or "union with the state of a particular religious society" was characterized "by giving its members exclusive political rights, and by compelling attendance of those who rejected its communion upon its worship or religious observances."

In selecting chaplains, Congress took no action liable to objection on establishment grounds—so described. According to the report: "[I]n this, no religion, no form of faith, no denomination of religious preferences, is established, in preference to any other, or has any peculiar privileges conferred upon it." Did the Senators here refer to chaplains who sought the lowest common denominational denominator—men who expressed no discernibly sectarian message? No: "Selections, in point of fact, are always made from some one of the denominations into which Christians are distributed."

The Senate committee report illustrates, too, the subtle but still decisive distinction involved in a legislative intent to promote the religious life of the people—where the people in fact are predominantly Christian—without affirming their religion to be true:

> This results from the fact that we are a Christian people—from the fact that almost our entire population belong to or sympathise with some one of the Christian denominations which compose the Christian world. And Christians will of course select, for the performance of religious services, one who professes the faith of Christ. This, however, it should be carefully noted, is not by virtue of provision, but voluntary choice. We are Christians, not because the law demands it, not to gain exclusive benefits, or to avoid legal disabilities, but from choice and education; and in a land thus universally Christian, what is to be expected, what desired

but that we shall pay a due regard to Christianity, and have a reasonable respect for it ministers and religious solemnities?[60]

The Senators affirmed that, where the reason for a law was the spiritual comfort and religious needs of some body of citizens, it should be their preferences ("voluntary choice") that settle the matter of which sort of spiritual comfort government should promote.

In their penultimate paragraph, the antebellum Senators most clearly affirmed the constitutional faith of their fathers. They held fast to inherited legal doctrines and to the overarching "natural religion" that they straightforwardly affirmed:

> Our fathers were true lovers of liberty, and utterly opposed to any constraint upon the rights of conscience. They intended, by this amendment, to prohibit "an establishment of religion" such as the English church presented, or anything like it. But they had no fear or jealousy of religion itself, nor did they wish to see us an irreligious people; they did not intend to prohibit a just expression of religious devotion by the legislators of the nation, even in their public character as legislators; they did not intend to send our armies and navies forth to do battle for the country without any national recognition of that God on whom success or failure depends; they did not intend to spread over all the public authorities and the whole public action of the nation the dead and revolting spectacle of atheistical apathy. Not so

---

60. *Senate Report No. 376*, 32nd Cong., 2nd Sess., 1.

had the battles of the revolution been fought, and the deliberations of the revolutionary Congress conducted. On the contrary, all had been done with a continual appeal to the Supreme Ruler of the world, and an habitual reliance upon His protection of the righteous cause which they commended to His care.

FRANKFURTER'S FOLLY (AND A BLACK MARK)

In 1948, in *McCollum v. Board of Education*,[61] Justice Felix Frankfurter concluded "that long before the Fourteenth Amendment subjected the states to new limitations, the prohibition of furtherance by the state of religious instruction became the guiding principle, in law and feeling, of the American people." The Fourteenth Amendment was ratified in 1868. Frankfurter thus asserted that within decades of the Founding ("long before 1868"), the American people had done an about-face from earlier practices.

What evidence did Frankfurter muster for this remarkable assertion? He cited Horace Mann's mid–19th century fight to bar sectarian teachings from common schools, saying that it was an exhortation to separate religion from education. A speech by President Ulysses Grant and the Blaine Amendment,[62] both seeking an end to public funding of "sectarian schools," demonstrated to Frankfurter that by 1875, "the sep-

---

[61.] *McCollum v. Board of Education*, 333 U.S. 203 (1948). One year after the *Everson* decision, the Court struck down a program—known as a "released-time program"—that allowed public school children to attend religious classes on school grounds. The Court struck down the program on the grounds that the use of classrooms for religious education violates the Establishment Clause.

aration...of the state from the teaching of religion, was firmly established in the consciousness of the nation."

Frankfurter's mistake is that these speakers meant what they said: a separation of sect from education. "Sect" was used basically with respect to Christianity and meant, as we have seen, something different from religion. Frankfurter overlooked, that is, the Founders' constitutional doctrines, which pivot upon this all-important distinction. The Founders spoke basically of sect and religion in relation to the state, whereas Frankfurter wants (or is wont) to speak of religion and secularism in relation to the state.

The mistake, if that is what it was, infected all that Frankfurter did with the historical evidence he examined. Contrary to what Frankfurter has him believe, Horace Mann affirmed "an education which instructed all children in the fundamental ethical norms which were the basis of all religions." In the words of one historian of American schooling, "No great educational leader before the Civil War...would tolerate any non-Christian beliefs in the schools."[63] Grant's speech had to do mainly with combating the growing practice of state support of private Catholic schools and had nothing to do with keep-

---

[62.] The Blaine Amendment, named after its proponent James G. Blaine, Speaker of the U.S. House in 1875, proposed that "No State shall make any law respecting an establishment of religion, or prohibiting the free exercise thereof; and no money raised by taxation in any state for the support of public schools, or derived from any public fund therefor, nor any public lands devoted thereto, shall ever be under the control of any religious sect; nor shall any money so raised or lands so devoted be divided between religious sects or denominations." The amendment passed the House of Representatives by a wide margin but failed by four votes to pass the supermajority vote needed in the Senate.

[63.] Merle Eugene Curti, *The Social Ideas of American Educators* (Patterson, N.J.: Pageant Books, Inc., 1959), 20.

ing religion out of public education. In fact, the version of the Blaine Amendment that was passed by the Senate expressly stipulated that its prohibitory language about "sectarian" schools should not be read to affect or prohibit the practice of Bible-reading in the schools.

The Blaine Amendment failed, but the idea did not wither and die. Many states, by now 37 in all, have state constitutional provisions similarly banning public financial aid to sectarian institutions. Many of these so-called baby Blaines were required by Congress; that is, several western states were required as a condition of their admission to the Union to insert into their initial state constitutions a Blaine-like ban on sectarian funding. (Among these is the Washington state provision that the Supreme Court upheld against a free exercise challenge in 2004 in *Locke v. Davey*.) The same free semantic substitution policy has undermined much of what the Court has said since 1947 about American history and the "separation of church and state."

Here is another example of how judicial inattention to the difference between *sect* and *religion* (purposeful or not) is subversive of historical instruction—as the terms have been used from the Founding forward. In *Zorach v. Clauson*,[64] the Court allowed public school authorities to release pupils early once a week, where parents requested it, to spend time in nearby religious schools studying doctrine. (Thus, it is called the "released time" case.) Justice Hugo Black dissented and as he usually did, whether in dissent or not, wrapped his argument

---

[64] *Zorach v. Clauson*, 343 U.S. 306 (1952). In another "released-time program" case, this time involving religious instruction off of school grounds, the Court upheld the program based on the facts that the religious education did not take place on school property, did not involve the use of public funds, and was not coercive.

in history. The substance of his dissent is a tissue of misconnects (with my commentary in brackets), such as:

> The Court's validation...rests in part upon its statement that Americans are "a religious people whose institutions presuppose a Supreme Being". [Correct] This was at least as true when the First Amendment was adopted; [correct] and it was just as true when eight Justices of this Court invalidated the released time system in *McCollum* [correct] on the premise that a state can no more "aid all religions" than it can aid one.

McCollum did adopt such a radical secularism, but how could the Founders' authority be mustered for that proposition in light of the deeply religious presuppositions that Black recognizes?

The "answer" lies in a Frankfurter-esque elision of *sect* with *religion*. Black asserted that 18th century Americans "were a religious people divided into many fighting sects"; that colonial history was replete with "zealous sectarians" who would "torture, maim and kill those they branded 'heretics', 'atheists' or 'agnostics'"; and that the First Amendment was "to insure that no one sect or combination of sects" could seize the government. But then Black leapt by *non sequitur* to the *coup de grace*: "Now as then, it is only by wholly isolating the state from the religious sphere" that the republic and religion can be saved. The possibility that Black never really considers is the one that the Founders adopted: If the problem has to do with sects, then the solution might have to do with them too, and not with the exclusion of religion generally.

OF "COOLIES" AND CLERGY

In an act passed in 1885, Congress forbade the importation of foreign contract workers. No domestic corporate entity or person was permitted to "prepay" or otherwise "assist or encourage" the importation of aliens "under contract or agreement" to perform "labor or service of any kind." From the submissions to and debate within Congress, it is clear that the law was intended only to curtail the importation of Chinese "coolies" and similar unskilled laborers. Then as now, imported laborers were supposed to be willing to work cheap, thus depressing the wages of native-born and already naturalized workers. The law's text, however, contained no such limitation. Its subject was imported contract labor as such.

E. Walpole Warren was an Anglican priest residing in England when Holy Trinity Church hired him as its pastor. He moved to New York City in 1887 pursuant to the agreement. The United States government claimed that his contract was void under the 1885 "coolie" law. The Supreme Court disagreed. Despite the fact that Warren's arrangement fell within the clear terms of the law, the Court declined to permit its application to him.

The Court's reasoning is no model of statutory construction. In *A Matter of Interpretation*, Justice Antonin Scalia described *Holy Trinity* as the "prototypical case involving the triumph of supposed 'legislative intent' (a handy cover for judicial intent) over the text of the law."[65] This may be true. Our interest for the moment, however, is not in normative canons of judicial behavior. Our concern is for what *Holy*

[65.] Justice Antonin Scalia, *A Matter of Interpretation: Federal Courts and the Law* (Princeton, N.J.: Princeton University Press, 1997), 18.

Trinity tells us about the turn-of-the-century health of the Founders' settlement.

The Court stated apodictically that "no purpose of action against religion can be imputed to *any* legislation, *state or national,* because this is a religious people" (emphasis added). The lengthy majority opinion by the deeply religious David Brewer sought to prove the proposition by canvassing (among many other pertinent sources) the Northwest Ordinance. The Court also "examine[d] the constitutions of various states." Every one of them, Brewer reported for a unanimous Court, "contains language which either directly or by clear implication recognizes a profound reverence for religion and an assumption that its influence in human affairs is essential to the well-being of the community."

The *Holy Trinity* Court also quoted with apparent approval another court opinion, this one from a Missouri case. The Missouri opinion as excerpted in *Holy Trinity* shows continuing understanding of and devotion to the Founders' settlement and to the pivotal distinction ignored by Justices Black and Frankfurter (among others). The Missouri case had to do with the founding documents of a college and the original intent to exclude "special or denominational religious influence." The Supreme Court then quoted this language: "We do not, hence, suppose that the founders intended to exclude all influence from, or instruction in, the great principles of Christian ethics, the basis of all character, the foundation of good citizenship and just government, and which are professedly adopted by men of all creeds."[66]

Holy Trinity closed with an interesting ecumenical appeal heralding an emerging stable pluralism. Brewer invited the reader to "suppose" that a Member of Congress in 1885

---

66. 151 U.S. at 655.

offered a bill that declared in specific terms that Cardinal Manning was not to contract with the Catholic Church in America to serve as pastor, "or any Baptist Church should make similar arrangements with Rev. Mr. Spurgeon; or any Jewish synagogue with some eminent Rabbi." "Can it be believed," Brewer challenged, "that [such a bill would win] a minute of approving thought or a single vote?"

FUNDING FAITH

After *Holy Trinity* and before the secularizing 1947 decision in *Everson*, the Supreme Court decided three challenges to government payments to religious groups. In each case, the expenditure was upheld. In *Bradfield v. Roberts*,[67] *Quick Bear v. Leupp*,[68] and *Cochran v. Board of Education*,[69] the Court indicated that so long as the main reason for a law was not to advance a sect, the incidental advancement of a sect did not violate the Establishment Clause. Government action with the incidental effect of supporting or advancing religion was constitutionally acceptable.

The flip side of this tolerance for promoting the sects is visible in *Reynolds*. Free exercise itself did not compel exceptions from an otherwise valid law (in *Reynolds*, one prohibiting polygamy) where the incidental effect was to inhibit religious

---

[67] *Bradfield v. Roberts*, 175 U.S. 291 (1899). Commissioners of D.C., pursuant to a congressional appropriation of funds, gave financial support to the directors of Providence Hospital. A private taxpayer sought to enjoin the support on the grounds that the hospital was composed of a monastic order of the Roman Catholic Church and thus constituted an establishment of religion. Passing over the question of taxpayer standing, Justice Rufus Peckham dismissed the Establishment Clause challenge because the act incorporating the hospital did not refer to religion: "Nothing is said about religion or about the religious faith of the incorporators of this institution in the act of incorporation."

practice. Legislators could recognize such an incidental effect and make allowance for it, as they commonly did in exempting "peace church" members from military or militia service, but nothing in the First Amendment required courts to craft exceptions.

In a splendid article, Professor Phil Hamburger concludes that "late 18th Century Americans...did not authorize or acknowledge a general constitutional right of religious exemption from civil laws."[70] Hamburger shows how "Americans reconciled their distaste for a [general] right of exemption with their support for religious freedom" and with their support for limited exemptions from specific obligations such as witness oath and military service.[71]

[68.] *Quick Bear v. Leupp*, 210 U.S. 50 (1908). The government made payments to sectarian missionaries operating schools on Indian reservations. The Court upheld the practice against an Establishment Clause challenge by noting that the appropriations for support came from tribal funds and not from public funds: "From the history of appropriations of public moneys for education of Indians, set forth in the brief of counsel for appellees, and again at length in the answer, it appears that before 1895 the government, for a number of years, had made contracts for sectarian schools for the education of the Indians, and the money due on these contracts was paid, in the discretion of the Commissioner of Indian Affairs, from the 'tribal funds' and from the gratuitous public appropriations."

[69.] *Cochran v. Louisiana State Board of Education*, 281 U.S. 370 (1930). This case involved a state law authorizing local school boards to purchase textbooks for all students, including parochial school students. Since the Establishment Clause had not yet been "incorporated," the issue was not establishment but whether the practice violated the 14th Amendment and due process by appropriating public money for private purposes. The Court upheld the state law on the basis that it gives a general benefit to the state to have all children educated with textbooks.

The following is a summary of this free exercise tradition from an ante-bellum Pennsylvania case quoted with approval by the Supreme Court in 1961:

> The constitution of this state secures freedom of conscience and equality of religious right. No man, living under the protection of our institutions, can be coerced to profess any form of religious belief, or to practise any peculiar mode of worship, in preference to another. In this respect, the Christian, the Jew, the Mohammedan, and the Pagan, are like entitled to protection. Nay, the Infidel, who madly rejects all belief in a Divine Essence, may safely do so, in reference to civil punishment, so long as he refrains from the wanton and malicious proclamation of his opinions with intent to outrage the moral and religious convictions of a community, the vast majority of whom are Christians. But beyond this, conscientious doctrines and practices can claim no immunity from the operation of general laws made for the government and to promote the welfare of the whole people.[72]

---

70. Philip A. Hamburger, "A Constitutional Right of Religious Exemption: An Historical Perspective," 60 *George Washington Law Review* 915, 916–917.

71. *Ibid.*, 916.

72. See *Specht v. Commonwealth*, 8 Pa. 312 (1848).

Chapter 4

THE SUPREME COURT ABANDONS THE FOUNDERS' DESIGN

$\mathcal{T}$he Supreme Court handed down a startling ruling on February, 10, 1947. *Everson v. Ewing Township Board of Education* involved a New Jersey township law which reimbursed parents for the cost of sending their children by bus to private schools, many of which were Catholic. The payments were upheld by a closely divided Court (5–4), essentially on *Cochran*-like grounds. *Everson* was not, according to the majority, really a matter of state assistance to religious institutions. It was really a case of including more rather than fewer children within the ambit of a public safety measure. Any aid to religion was incidental and attenuated.

Cochran was an especially apt precedent because, like *Everson*, it involved a state expenditure. Going into the *Everson* case, the First Amendment Establishment Clause did not apply to the activities of the state governments. That is why *Cochran* had been a due process case and why *Everson* was expected to be one too. The whole Bill of Rights had long been held to inhibit the activities of the national government only. Federal prosecutions, for example, had to be commenced by indictment, and federal civil cases had to be tried before a jury, according to the Fifth and Seventh Amendments, respectively. But states were at liberty to lodge criminal charges by prosecutor's complaint or police accusation and were under no constitutional obligation to empanel grand juries at all. States were free to try civil matters before a judge without a jury.[73]

The Supreme Court began applying Bill of Rights provisions to the states in the 1920s, starting with freedom of speech and freedom of the press. In the early 1940s and in cases involving prosecutions of Jehovah's Witnesses for disturbing the peace or for illegal door-to-door soliciting or distribution of handbills, the Court melded its prior "incorporation" for freedom of speech and press with free exercise.[74] The new compound amounted to a federal constitutional right against state or national infringement of one's right to freedom of expression.

One startling thing about *Everson*, then, was its declaration that the Establishment Clause was "incorporated" and therefore applied to the states just as it had previously applied to the national government. The move was both unexpected and ironic: unexpected because *Everson* had neither been briefed nor argued as an Establishment Clause dispute and ironic because

---

73. They still are. The Fifth Amendments' indictment requirement is among the few Bill of Rights provisions that have never been "incorporated"—that is, applied to the states.

74. See, for example, *Prince v. Massachusetts*, 321 U.S. 158 (1944), where a Jehovah's Witness was convicted for violating child labor laws for having her nine-year-old daughter distribute religious literature on the street. The woman claimed that her right to free exercise was violated by this conviction. The Court upheld her conviction because the law is general and (peculiarly) because the violation of the law took place in public—meaning that the violation of free exercise might be more plausible if government was condemning certain things done in private.

Everson v. Board of Education, 330 U.S. 1 (1947)

Facts of the Case: The Board of Education of Ewing Township, authorized by a New Jersey statute, adopted a busing plan that reimbursed parents for transporting their children to private schools on regular public buses. A large portion of this money went to parents to pay for transportation of children to Catholic parochial schools.

Decision: In a 5-4 decision, the Supreme Court upheld the New Jersey statute and the busing plan, ruling that it did not violate the Establishment Clause as applied to the states through the Fourteenth Amendment.

Majority Opinion: Writing for the Court, Justice Hugo Black asserted that the Establishment Clause is "incorporated" by the Fourteenth Amendment and thus applies to the states as well as Congress. He interpreted the meaning of the Establishment Clause in light of Thomas Jefferson's famous metaphor of the "wall of separation" between church and state, writing that "[t]he First Amendment has erected a wall between church and state. That wall must be kept high and impregnable. We could not approve the slightest breach." After staking the claim that the Establishment Clause is extremely hostile to religion, however, Justice Black claimed that "New Jersey has not breached" this high wall and that the practice in question is constitutional.

Dissenting Opinion: The dissent disagreed with the majority's claim that "New Jersey has not breached" the wall. Applying the majority's reasoning, the dissent argued that the "wall" was "breached" by the payment of taxpayer money to support religious education and that the statute and plan were unconstitutional.

Significance: The Court's opinion yielded three important results. First, the Court applied the Establishment Clause for the first time against state governments as well as Congress. Second, the Court claimed that *any* government support or preference for religion is equivalent to an unconstitutional establishment. As the Court said, the Establishment Clause means that states cannot "pass laws which aid one religion, aid all religions, or prefer one religion over another." Third, in making this argument, the Court relied on Jefferson's famous "wall of separation" metaphor, which has come to replace the actual text of the Establishment Clause in the public mind.

the Establishment Clause was intended in part precisely to preserve state autonomy from national interference in religious matters.

The other startling thing is what the Court said the Establishment Clause meant: Public authorities at the state and federal levels could not promote, encourage, or aid religion, even where there was no coercion or discrimination among religious bodies. There could be no preference for religion over nonreligion. The Court said that this secularist manifest was the unequivocal command of the Founders.

Where did this revolutionary declaration come from? Justice Black's opinion for the *Everson* Court went through several drafts, with at least three doctrinal leaps along the way. At first, Black would have ruled in favor of the reimbursement law on the strength of *Cochran*. Under pressure from separationist brethren, he then "incorporated" the Establishment Clause. Black wrote in that draft, however, that non-establishment required equality among religions. Finally, Black circulated the opinion that went into the books and set out the unprecedented secularist mandate: The Establishment Clause, Black wrote for the Court, "mean[t] at least" that neither the states nor the federal government could "aid one religion, aid all religions, or prefer one religion over another.... [T]he state [must] be neutral in its relations with groups of religious believers and non-believers."[75] The Court also declared that "no tax large or small can be levied to support any religious activities or institutions."[76]

The Founders' distinction between sect and natural religion is absent from *Everson*. The case contains not a word of approval for religion as the main theme of the "missing

---

[75] 330 U.S. at 15.

[76] *Ibid.*

Federalist Paper." Quite the contrary: The Court said for the first time what it would say often beginning in the 1960s: Not a penny for religion, lest the principle of strict separation (read: secularism) be compromised with the inevitable consequence that the warring sects would plunder the public treasury and imperil the republic. Justice Wiley Rutledge, in his *Everson* dissent, said this.[77]

In *Schempp* (1963), the Court emphasized that it was "no defense to urge that the religious practices here may be relatively minor encroachments on the First Amendment." What is today a "trickling stream," the Court later added in *Nyquist* (1973), may be a torrent tomorrow.[78] The underlying view of believers' motives when civically engaged is hardly flattering or accurate. The Court's conviction that the public benefits of religion—if any there be—are not worth the toll is nonetheless clear.

The *Everson* Court told a long and colorful story of "freedom-loving colonials," but the story is purely "Whig history." "Whig history" has nothing to do with phony hair or defunct political parties. It is a term used to describe historical accounts (on any subject) that depict human events marching steadily forward to an enlightened present. In his *The Whig Interpretation of History*, Herbert Butterfield wrote of "the tendency of many historians to write on the side of Protestants and Whigs, to praise revolutions provided they have been successful, to emphasize certain principles of progress in the past and to produce a story which is the ratification if not the glorification of the present."[79] A "Whig history" treats the present as synthesis of all that was good in the past and the

---

77. 330 U.S at 40–41.
78. 413 U.S. at n. 56.
79. Herbert Butterfield, *The Whig Interpretation of History*, reprint (New York: W.W. Norton & Company, 1965), v.

past as "a grand ascent to the pinnacle of the present—namely, ourselves."[80]

Justice Black attributed to his "freedom-loving colonials" the strict separation that he favored but which was scarcely fathomable, much less appealing, to the Founders. Black relied strategically on the authority of just one "freedom-loving colonial": James Madison. In his opinion for the Court, however, he did not rely on anything Madison said or did in connection with the First Amendment. Instead, Black featured a circular composed by Madison in 1785–1786 for use in a Virginia struggle over tax support of religion teachers—the *Memorial and Remonstrance.*

Madison's petition deserves notice in any account of the Founders' understanding of religious liberty, but the *Everson* Court overstated the place of Madison's omnibus circular in the Virginia struggle and never explained what it had to do with the matter at hand: the meaning of the First Amendment to the Constitution. Black simply asserted (without evidence) that the Virginia debate and Madison's *Memorial and Remonstrance* were "warp and woof" of the First Amendment.[81]

So marked the start of a trend. In a 1995 decision, Justice David Souter asserted that Madison's petition played "the central role" in defeating the Virginia bill and "framed the debate upon which the Religion Clauses stand."[82] In the 2005 Ten Commandments cases, the majority struck down a Kentucky courthouse display of the Decalogue, relying upon the *Memorial*

---

80. See John D. Mueller, "The Return of Natural-Law Economics," presented at the Colloquium on the American Founding, Amherst University, October 19, 2002, p. 4; available at *www.lehrmaninstitute.org/policy/muller_oct02.pdf.*

81. *Everson v. Board of Education,* 330 U.S. 1 (1947), 39.

82. *Ronald v. Rosenberger, et al. v. Rector and Visitors of the University of Virginia,* 515 U.S. 819 (1995), 868.

Lee v. Weisman, 505 U.S. 577 (1992)

Facts of the Case: At an 1989 middle school graduation ceremony, Rabbi Leslie Gutterman offered an invocation prayer, participation in which was voluntary. Daniel Weisman, parent of a child present at the ceremony, sued school officials, alleging that mentioning God during public school graduation ceremonies violates the Establishment Clause. Weisman won in federal district court and the First Circuit Court of Appeals, and the case was appealed to the Supreme Court.

Decision: In a 5-4 decision, the Court ruled that the prayer violated the Establishment Clause.

Majority Opinion: Although participation in the prayer was voluntary, Justice Anthony Kennedy argued on behalf of the Court that "public pressure, as well as peer pressure, on attending students to stand as a group or, at least, maintain respectful silence during the Invocation and Benediction...can be as real as any overt compulsion." Therefore, the school district's prayer was coercive, and students were psychologically compelled to participate: "[T]he State, in a school setting, in effect required participation in a religious exercise."

Dissenting Opinion: Writing in dissent and joined by Chief Justice William Rehnquist and Associate Justices Byron White and Clarence Thomas, Justice Antonin Scalia condemned the majority opinion for striking down a practice that "is a component" of a "longstanding American tradition of nonsectarian prayer to God at public celebrations generally." Scalia particularly criticized the majority's "instrument of destruction" in this case, the "test of psychological coercion," as "psychology practiced by amateurs."

Significance: The decision supported the trend of previous Supreme Court precedents that had severely restricted public support of religion in schools and public buildings. It also changed the legal landscape by using a new "coercion test" rather than the previously established *Lemon* test to determine Establishment Clause cases.

and Remonstrance for the meaning of the Establishment Clause,[83] and that decision cited the Court's earlier reliance in *Lee v. Weisman*, a 1992 case ruling a public school graduation prayer unconstitutional.

In truth, Madison's broadside played a modest role in the Virginia fight over tax support of teachers of the Christian religion. Just one-fifth of all Virginians who signed petitions against the tax signed Madison's. Many Virginians who favored government aid to religion also voted against the bill. They could not afford the proposed assessment. Even Justice Rutledge, who dissented in *Everson* on ultra-strict separationist grounds, conceded there that poverty was a contributing factor in the assessment's defeat.

Justice Black invited readers of his *Everson* opinion to conclude that because Madison (and Jefferson) opposed the assessment, prominent Virginians generally opposed it, but this is simply inaccurate. On the Madisonian or anti-assessment side of the political ledger, one should add George and Wilson Nicholas; George Mason, who attended the Philadelphia Convention in 1787; and Andrew Moore, a member of the First Congress, which proposed the Establishment Clause to the states for ratification. On the side that supported tax assessments for the teaching of the Christian religion were George Washington; John Marshall; Patrick Henry, the most powerful politician in Virginia at the time; then-Governor Benjamin Harrison; Edward Pendleton; Edmund Randolph, Attorney General in the Washington Administration; John Page, a colleague of Madison's in the First Congress; John Frances Mercer, another delegate to the 1787 Convention; and one of Virginia's first Senators, Richard Henry Lee. Clearly in agreement with the bill's principle because of their contempo-

---

83. See *McCreary County v. ACLU*, 125 S. Ct. 2722 (2005), 2744.

raneous support of a different aid-to-religion bill were Virginia's other Senator, William Grayson, and the fifth President of the United States, James Monroe.

Early in the controversy, Senator Lee shared with Madison his pro-assessment rationale:

> Refiners may weave as fine a web of reason as they please, but the experience of all times shews Religion to be the guardian of morals—and he must be a very inattentive observer in our Country, who does not see that avarice is accomplishing the destruction of religion, for want of a legal obligation to contribute something to its support. The declaration of rights [in the Virginia Constitution], it seems to me, rather contends against forcing modes of faith and forms of worship, than against compelling contribution for the support of religion in general.[84]

Lee succinctly expressed the main points of the Founders' settlement: constitutional protection against government-enforced "faith" and "worship" (matters that distinguished the sects); a common good in "religion" to which all would be made to contribute because all benefited from its support; and the "missing *Federalist Paper*."

It is important to note the variety of sources that fueled the secularist pressure in *Everson*. Some sources were peculiar to a justice; others were part of ideologies and prejudices in the air. Justice Black, for example, had been a member of the Ku Klux Klan earlier in his political career, and his Supreme Court nomination nearly foundered upon that association. Justice

---

[84.] Richard Henry Lee, Letter to James Madison, 26 November 1784, in 2 *Letters of Richard Henry Lee*, 304.

Felix Frankfurter was among the most secular-minded individuals ever to sit on the Court. Justice William O. Douglas was a fiercely independent soul to whom organized religion was a yoke upon mind and spirit. He regularly sprinkled his church–state opinions with anti-Catholic diatribes. Justice Wiley Rutledge grew up in an anti-Catholic Baptist household in which his father once said that he would "vote for the blackest man in Africa before voting for Al Smith."[85]

There was a sizable concern on the Court (and among many off the Court) for the growing political and cultural power of the Catholic Church. During the *Everson* oral argument, Douglas passed a note to Black that read: "If the Catholics get public money to finance their religious schools, we better insist on getting some good prayers in public schools or we Protestants are out of business."[86] Following the initial conference of the justices, Rutledge drew up a frankly worded memo to the same effect. "We all know," he wrote, "that this is really a fight by the Catholic schools to secure this money from the public treasury. It is aggressive and on a wide scale. The worst thing that could happen to this country would be to throw its religious demands, financially speaking, into politics."[87]

But there was more to the justices' concerns than rank prejudice. Their "prejudice" against religion—especially against Catholicism—was also the negative implication of more positive philosophical and political beliefs. Frankfurter

---

85. Cited in John M. Ferren, *Salt of the Earth, Conscience of the Court: The Story of Justice Wiley Rutledge* (Chapel Hill: University of North Carolina Press, 2004), 17.

86. Del Dickson, ed., *The Supreme Court in Conference (1940–1985)* (Oxford University Press, 2001), 401, n. 26.

87. Cited in John T. McGreevy, *Catholicism and American Freedom: A History* (W.W. Norton & Co., 2003), 185.

said at the *Everson* conference that the Court's "new trend" of decisions had already "shifted [its] latest views about our democracy."[88] In those cases, the Court had established the priority of individual freedom of expression over the alleged requirements of peace and order.

These cases evince that the Court was engaged in a reconsideration of what we have called the "missing *Federalist Paper*." The Founders wondered aloud whether a "republican" government could somehow call forth (or cultivate or inculcate) sufficient virtue in the people. By the Second World War's end, the overarching political form was not "republic" but "democracy," and its requirements went well beyond "virtue" to include—even to make primary—intelligence and information. *Everson* continued this development.

What was that "new" set of "views about democracy"? There was a fork in the trail of democratic theory. One account of democracy held that it depended upon a citizenry possessed of moral truth. The other camp of democrats saw moral truth as a phantom, a superstition that, if it seized hold of citizens' minds, led straight to authoritarianism if not fascism. These people favored a pragmatic philosophical spirit, relativism in morals, and a free market in ideas.

This latter group found favor on the Supreme Court. Justice Jackson tellingly wrote in his *Thomas v. Collins* concurrence that "it cannot be the duty, because it is not the right, of the state to protect the public against false doctrine."[89] The term "doctrine" was not limited to theological speculation. As Jackson used the word, it gathered

---

88. Dickson, ed., *The Supreme Court in Conference*, 400.

89. *Thomas v. Collins*, 323 U.S. 516, 545 (1945). The Court held that a Texas law requiring labor union organizers to obtain a permit prior to soliciting potential members is an unconstitutional violation of freedom of speech.

meaning from a set of antonyms: free speech, free press, *and* freedom of religion. In all these matters, "every person must be his own watchman for truth."[90]

The *Thomas* Court said that the whole First Amendment was comprised of "indispensable democratic freedoms." Even the corporate proprietor of a town full of employee residents and their families could not limit free citizens' access to the information and ideas that, according to the Court, they needed to make democracy work. "To act as good citizens [these people too] must be informed. In order to enable them to be properly informed their information must be uncensored"—even by the private corporate owner of the "company town."[91]

Broadening our look at this developing constellation of ideas about the relationship of our political form—described now as "democracy"—to the character of citizens, especially with reference to religion, we see something revolutionary afoot. In the mid-1940s, the Court confronted—or, rather, constructed—an unprecedented problem concerning religion and democracy. Terms such as "orthodox," "dogma," "secularism," "irreligion, "no religion," "atheism," "inculcate," and "indoctrinate" were rarely to be found in the Court's opinions going back to 1790; after around 1943, these terms became prevalent, marking no less than an epistemological revolution on the Court. Since then, these words have become synonyms for the teaching of religion, which the Court has invariably viewed as bypassing students' critical reasoning and freedom of choice.

The evidence shows that during and after the war, our political form—"democracy"—was the fount from which

90. *Ibid.*
91. 326 U.S. at 508.

flowed the justices' conceptions of the "first freedoms." The definition of religious liberty was no longer derived from the Constitution's text, the Founders' understanding of and their aims for it, or the tradition of constitutional interpretation by courts and other leading lights. Religious liberty was instead an effect of contemporary political theorizing.

Central to the new understanding was the Court's denial of epistemic authority to the state: The democratic state, like Pontius Pilate, did not know and thus could not enforce "truth." Another critical part of the "new" construct was the Court's denial to the state of any authority to affirm, endorse, or otherwise vouch for the authority of religion ("neutral between religion and non-religion"). In *West Virginia State Board of Education v. Barnette,* the Court said that even "things that touch the heart of the existing order" could not be settled as true by government.[92] But they could be—and were settled— by virtue of being *ours*—"our democratic way of life" was at least authoritative and the highest normative appeal available within reflection upon what do about matters of state and law. Whether it was true and what else that might exactly mean were not particularly important questions.

Everson was so shockingly secular in *dictum*[93] that observers wondered whether the Court really meant it. After all, the case had not gone to the Court as a vehicle for sweeping change in matters fundamental, and the outcome of the particular decision was pro-religion: The Catholic school children and

---

92. *West Virginia State Board of Education v. Barnette,* 319 U.S. 624 (1943). In what was technically a free speech case, the Court ruled that the state cannot force Jehovah's Witnesses or other citizens to salute the flag. The Court did not talk about free exercise and religious beliefs but applied the ruling broadly by saying that the state does not have the power to compel this behavior.

93. In other words, the Court's pronouncement on an interpretive matter extraneous to the case.

their parents won. What was going on? The *McCollum* case slated for the next term loomed as the real test of what the Court had wrought.

McCollum v. Board of Education came from Champaign, Illinois, location of the state's flagship university campus. The controversy involved the local school authority's practice of permitting local clergymen to enter the schools weekly to instruct the children of consenting parents in their respective faiths. One parent who did not want her son to be instructed—and who was not satisfied with the arrangement (basically, idle study hall) for her boys, sued.

The oral argument in *McCollum* took place just 10 months after the shocking *Everson* declaration against any and all government help to religion even if the help was non-discriminatory and non-coercive. Frankfurter made this point to John Franklin, the very able lawyer for the Champaign, Illinois, school board, which had opened its classrooms to voluntary religious instruction by local clergy:

> I put my question again: we have a school system of the United States on the one hand, and the relation it has to the democratic way of life. On the other hand we have the religious beliefs of our people. The question is whether any kind of scheme which introduced religious teaching into the public school system is the kind of thing we should have in our democratic institutions.[94]

Justice Black wrote for the Court again, this time for a majority of eight. He offered no refutation or rejoinder, no rebuttal or counterargument, to Franklin. In full, the Court's response to Franklin's case was: "We are unable to accept th[e]

[94.] See 5 *Engage: The Journal of the Federalist Society's Practice Groups*, 131, 145 (2004).

argument. As we stated in *Everson* we must keep the wall high and impregnable."

The nation's religious leaders responded to *McCollum* as a clarion call to action. A typical response is recorded in John McGreevy's *Catholicism and American Freedom*. McGreevy himself asserts that *McCollum* "erected a putative 'wall of separation' between church and state." He reports on an "off-the-record meeting of religious leaders held in the wake" of the decision. At one *McCollum* postmortem meeting, John Courtney Murray, one of the leading American Catholic intellectuals of that (or any other) time, "emphasized that the *McCollum* decision was a victory for secularism and as such should be of great concern to Catholics, Jews and Protestants."[95] It was.

Religion got its revenge less than four years later with a boost from Joe Stalin. The Cold War recast the Court's understanding of our polity's relationship to God by making an enemy of our former ally: the menacing specter of atheistic Communism.

---

[95] McGreevy, *Catholicism and American Freedom*, 205.

Chapter 5

THE SECULARIZATION PROJECT TAKES A BREAK

*T*he 1951 term was uncharacteristically eventful for religion. Then the Court went silent for a decade.[96] When finally aroused from its slumber, the Court embarked upon its *Engel* revolution.

In 1952, the Court decided *Zorach v. Clausen*, the "released time" case from New York City. "Released time" usually arrived on Wednesday afternoons, but whenever it took place, public school children were "released" early—at parental request—to receive religious instruction at a nearby parochial school. "Released time" was almost wholly used by Catholics, though no legal restriction made it so. No religious instruction occurred on public property, but public school authorities kept records, supervised early dismissal, tolerated "down time"

[96.] Except for *Kedroff v. St. Nicholas Cathedral*, decided in 1953. In *Kedroff*, the Court held that the Free Exercise Clause included a broad freedom of churches to select clergy without interference. The Court struck down New York legislation that attempted to protect the American branch of the Russian Orthodox Church from Muscovite control. After that, and notwithstanding a host of *cert* petitions and appeals each term, there were no significant church–state decisions until *McGowan* upheld Sunday blue laws in May 1961. See note 104, *infra*.

while the students were absent, and otherwise promoted what amounted to catechetical instruction.

In an opinion written by Justice Douglas, the Court sustained "released time." The *Zorach* Court said that there "cannot be the slightest doubt that the First Amendment reflects the philosophy that Church and State should be separated." That amendment, "however, does not say that in every and all respects there shall be '"separation."'" Instead, "it studiously defines the manner, the specific ways, in which there shall be no concert or union or dependency one on the other." This is "common sense." "Otherwise the state and religion would be aliens to each other—hostile, suspicious, and even unfriendly." Black, Frankfurter, and Jackson dissented.

Zorach was unmistakably at odds with the separationist doctrine of *McCollum* and *Everson*. *Zorach*'s "accommodationism"—as it swiftly came to be called—became the law of the land. The Supreme Court did nothing to diminish its authority for the rest of the decade, although it also said little to emphasize or reinforce *Zorach*'s testimony to natural theology's role in the republic. And the law on the ground—that made and applied by all the other courts in the land—soon forgot the Court's aborted attempt, in *McCollum* and *Everson*, to strip the public square naked.

Zorach did not expressly overrule *McCollum*, but lower courts could scarcely reconcile the two cases. *Everson* was much less of an issue. The precise result of the case—thumbs-up for parochial school expenses—was compatible with *Zorach*'s "accommodationism," and *Everson*'s expansive language otherwise could be—and would have been, save for *McCollum*—treated as *dictum*. By the time the Supreme Court decided *Engel v. Vitale* in 1962, the verdict of the lower courts was in: *Zorach* was the law and *McCollum* was not.

Cases coming after *Zorach* characteristically viewed *Everson*'s expansive language as mere *dictum.* These subsequent cases by and large zeroed in on *Everson*'s holding in favor of aid to religious education, limited *McCollum* to its facts, and took *Zorach*'s accommodationism to be the controlling principle of federal constitutional law.

The *Engel* case on first appeal[97] held that an optional prayer before class was constitutional. As in several other cases, the court treated *Zorach* as a way to break down the strict separation between church and state, thus further confining *Everson.* Introducing a long passage from *Zorach*, the court claimed that the *Zorach* majority "gave to the nation these basic principles for its guidance." It would seem, then, that by 1960 the authority of *Everson* had significantly eroded. Few federal appellate and state supreme courts feared being overturned for failing to follow, or even cite, *Everson.*

Two laws enacted by Congress in 1954 witness to the tradition of religion in America. Each put in place a practice that today's American would probably say is actually much older, perhaps even a Founders' antique. One law put the National Motto—In God We Trust—on all currency. The other added to the Pledge of Allegiance the words "under God." In each instance, legislators cited *Zorach* in support and as an illustration of what they were doing. Sponsors of each bill quoted the Court's declaration in *Zorach* that "[w]e are a religious people whose institutions presuppose a Supreme Being."[98]

These were not idle bromides or thoughtlessly repeated platitudes. The Cold War (then so recently aflame in Korea) eliminated the possibility of complacency about our freedoms.

[97.] 206 N.Y.S.2d 183 (Ct. App. 1960).

[98.] *See U.S. Code Congressional and Administrative News*, 83rd Cong., 2nd Sess (1954), 2340.

As the House report in favor of amending the Pledge observed:

> At this moment in our history the principles underlying our American government and the American way of life are under attack by a system whose philosophy is at direct odds with our own.... [Inclusion of "under God"] would serve to deny the atheistic and materialistic concepts of communism with its attendant subservience of the individual.[99]

Or, as the sponsors of "In God We Trust" exclaimed during House hearings: "[T]he one fundamental issue which is the unbridgeable gap between America and Communist Russia is belief in Almighty God."

Perhaps some of the less devout went quietly along with these exclamations, reasoning that the enemy (God) of my enemy (Russia) must be my friend. There is no reason to doubt, though, the sincerity of those who—quite remarkably, it would soon seem to many—saw in public religion the only sure way to preserve human rights and individuality. "[P]rinciples of the worthwhileness of the individual human being are meaningless unless there exists a Supreme Being."[100] But these enactments nonetheless stand for the "natural theology" of the Declaration of Independence. As the House committee said:

> Our American Government is founded on the concept of the individuality and the dignity of the human being. Underlying this concept is the belief that the human person is important because he was created by God and endowed by

---

99. *Ibid.*

100. *Ibid.*

him with certain inalienable rights which no civil authority may usurp. The inclusion of God in our pledge would further acknowledge the dependence of our people and our government upon the moral directions of the Creator.[101]

A further illustration of the 1950s' revival of the Founders' settlement is a story told during consideration of the Pledge bill. President Eisenhower joined with Bishop Fulton J. Sheen, Dr. Norman Vincent Peale, Rabbi Norman Salit, and American Legion Commander Arthur J. Connell in the American Legion's "Back to God" appeal in connection with its Four Chaplains' Day, commemorating the four military chaplains who heroically gave their lives when the troop ship *Dorchester* was sunk in 1943. The President declared that "all the history of America" bears witness to the truth that "in time of test or trial we instinctively turn to God." "Today, as then [Gettysburg], there is need for positive acts of renewed recognition that faith is our surest...strength, our greatest resource."[102]

It is certainly fair to wonder about the continuity and discontinuity of church–state jurisprudence from the mid-1940s through (as we shall see in the next chapter) the early 1960s. It surely seems that the Court rocked back and forth wildly without apparent justification or explanation. In fact, the Court has been loathe to overrule frankly any of its Establishment Clause cases, so much so that irreconcilable holdings remain on the books—and so much so that the untrained eye glancing at the cases collected in the U.S. Reports might believe what the Court publicly professes: The

---

[101.] *Ibid.*

[102.] 2 *U.S. Code Congressional and Administrative News*, 83rd Cong., 2nd Sess (1954), 2341.

cases really are one long line of consistent holdings. Except that the naive reader sooner or later happens upon a moment of judicial candor. One such moment was Chief Justice Warren Burger's confession that the "wall of separation" had become by 1973 a "blurred, indistinct and variable barrier." This may have been an understatement.

We can see through the bombastic rhetoric of the cases that the Court's detour away from the original meaning of the First Amendment is rooted in novel thinking by the Court's members, but "novel" in the limited sense of being unprecedented in the Court's decisions. No doubt the adventurous justices were retailing the ideas of scholars and journalists off the Court (such as Black's reliance upon the work of Charles Beard). The question thus arises about the 1950s' return to tradition: Was it a true restoration of what the Founders had wrought for that reason? Or was it the case that political exigencies particular to the 1950s—the Cold War—steered the Court onto traditional terrain?

Chapter 6

THE COURT
REVIVES SECULARISM

Secularism was at the top of the *Engel* petitioners' agenda. Their lawyer, William Butler, came before the Court to preserve religious liberty. He said so at oral argument. The only way to do that, he urged upon the Court, was to "keep religion out of our public life." Later in the argument, Butler was asked by a justice unidentified in the transcript: "[I]s it your position that our public schools, by virtue of our Constitution, are frankly secular institutions?" He answered: "Absolutely yes." That was his "ultimate position," Butler added emphatically.

Butler's candor was not a *kamikaze* tactic or a naive protest. The Supreme Court had secularism on its mind too—again. The Court had signaled in two cases decided 10 months earlier that the decade-long revival of church–state cooperation was ending. In *Torcaso v. Watkins*, the Court held that Maryland's "test oath" requirement for office violated the Establishment Clause.[103] In *McGowan v. Maryland*, the Court concluded that Sunday closing laws no longer enforced civil religious obligations.[104] A common day of rest and recreation served the public interest apart from any religious purpose, function, or effect. Therefore, they did not run afoul of the Free Exercise or Establishment Clauses because they were not religious in character.

But *Engel* was the real launch site for the Court's privatization project. In his argument, Butler relied "very heavily" (his words) on *McCollum*. He distinguished *Zorach* as an off-premises religious observance having no connection to the legal issue in the case.

The Court, save for Justice Potter Stewart, seemed to be on Butler's side. Stewart pressed him hard to distinguish the Regents' prayer—"Almighty God we acknowledge our dependence on Thee"—from "I pledge allegiance to…one nation under God." Butler faltered, as he also did when pressed to distinguish other divine adornments of public life: "in God We Trust," "God Save this Honorable Court," and the like.

Butler argued that informal social and psychological pressures combined to vitiate children's option not to participate in the Regents' prayer: that the prayer was really coerced. The Court would adopt this sort of offering in later school prayer cases such as *Lee v. Weisman*, speaking of children's susceptibility to "coercion" (i.e., peer pressure) around school that would make all education into indoctrination.[105] But not in *Engel*:

[103.] *Torcaso v. Watkins*, 367 U.S. 488 (1961). The Maryland Declaration of Rights states that no religious test shall be administered as a prerequisite for holding public office, except for a declaration of belief in the existence of God. The state required a declaration of belief in God, and Torcaso was denied his appointment to Notary Public of Maryland as a result of his refusal to make such a declaration. The Court unanimously declared that this was a violation of Torcaso's religious freedom, but it seemed to do so on Establishment Clause, not Free Exercise, grounds.

[104.] *McGowan v. Maryland*, 366 U.S. 420 (1961). Sunday closing laws that prohibited the sale of certain items on Sunday were upheld against a challenge that these laws amounted to a violation of the Establishment Clause. The Court ruled that the purpose of the law was to promote secular ends and that it therefore did not amount to such a violation.

Engel v. Vitale, 370 U.S. 421 (1962)

Facts of the Case: Steven Engel and other parents of students in the Union Free School District of Hyde Park, New York, sued the principal and Board of Education of that district, challenging the practice of opening each school day with a brief nonsectarian prayer to "Almighty God" in each class. They contended that this violated the First Amendment's Establishment Clause. The New York Court of Appeals ruled for the board, and Engel appealed to the Supreme Court.

Decision: The Supreme Court ruled 6-1 that the school-sponsored prayer violated the Establishment Clause as applied to the states through the Fourteenth Amendment.

Majority Opinion: Despite defendant's claims that the prayer was nonsectarian and that recitation was voluntary, Justice Hugo Black reasoned that by promoting religion, the practice violated the Establishment Clause even if the promotion in question was non-coercive. Justice Black granted that the prayer was non-denominational and that students were not compelled to recite, but he asserted that these facts were irrelevant because the prayer "officially establishes the beliefs embodied in the Regents' prayer," implicitly asserting that any support of religion by government is tantamount to an establishment of religion.

Dissenting Opinion: Justice Potter Stewart, the lone dissenter, argued that he could not "see how an 'official religion' is established by letting those who want to say a prayer say it." Stewart attacked the majority for ignoring the distinction between an establishment of religion and government support of religion or accommodation of religious practices in public settings. He stated that "we deal here not with the establishment of a state church" but merely with a voluntary prayer in an educational setting.

Significance: *Engel* subsequently became the basis for future decisions limiting government-directed prayer in school settings. It also marked a return to the Supreme Court's hostility to government support of religion at any level of government by reviving the reasoning of the pivotal *Everson* case and abandoning the trend of cases such as *Zorach v. Clauson.*

The *Engel* Court said unequivocally that *coercion* was not part of its reasoning.

Those defending the prayer made the contrast with Butler as clear as it could be made. Bertram Daiker represented local school officials, and he said: "[H]ere is where my friend [Butler] and I depart in our thinking. Since the earliest days of this country, going back to the Mayflower Compact, the men who put our country together have publicly and repeatedly recognized the existence of a Supreme Being, a God." Later on, Porter Chandler, standing up for intervening parents who favored the prayer, said that petitioners "are now seeking to...to eliminate all reference to God from the whole fabric of our public life and of our public educational system."

The *Engel* Court said that "neither the fact that the prayer may be denominationally neutral nor the fact that its observance on the part of the students is voluntary can serve to free it from the limitations of the Establishment Clause, as it might from the Free Exercise Clause." The reach and point of the Establishment Clause are broader. The point of that clause was to forestall "union" of government and religion, to leave "religious function[s] to the people themselves and to those the people choose to look to for religious guidance."[106] But should the people choose to look to public officials for such guidance, they are out of luck. The Establishment Clause expresses the "principle" that religion is "too personal, too sacred, too holy, to permit its 'unhallowed perversion' by a civil magistrate"[107]—except that "unhallowed perversion" was not a sorting tool. In other words, the Court's ruling made it clear that *whenever* the civil magistrate gets involved with religion, it *is* an "unhallowed perversion."

[105.] See *Lee v. Weisman*, inset.
[106.] *Engel v. Vitale*, 370 U.S. 421, 435.
[107.] *Ibid.* at 432.

Justice Stewart in dissent could not see "how an 'official religion' is established by letting those who want to say a prayer say it."[108] He had pressed Butler hard about the Pledge and now worked the problem into his opinion. The National Motto, the "Star-Spangled Banner," and "under God" were at stake. The validity of them all, Stewart asserted, was "summed up by this Court just ten years ago in a single sentence: 'We are a religious people whose institutions presuppose a Supreme Being.'"[109]

The *Engel* Court did not expressly overrule *Zorach*, but it did make a shambles of *Zorach's* reasoning. To *Zorach's* notion that secularism indicated hostility to religion, *Engel* replied: "Nothing, of course, could be more wrong."[110] Why? Probably because religion does not naturally or rightly manifest itself politically. Religion is private.

Zorach had been received by later courts as stating that "separation" was a matter of "degree." Prudential judgments about how far to go had to be made, but those judgments would presuppose that moderate cooperation and recognition of God were good things. No more: *Engel* set the tone for 22 years of judicial hyperscrupulousness by quoting Madison: "It is proper to take alarm at the first experiment on our liberties." The *principle* of separation could tolerate no exceptions because—as the Court said wholly without irony—steadfast consistency was the *only* alternative to persecution.

Engel's more formidable-looking arguments were facades. The first was another helping of historical fiction served up by the author of the *Everson* and *McCollum* opinions, Hugo Black. This was the oft-told tale of English persecution and intolerance (the historical part), which somehow (the fiction)

---

108. *Ibid.* at 445.
109. *Ibid.* at 450.
110. *Ibid.* at 434.

caused or would have caused the Founders to judge a voluntary nondenominational school prayer to be the camel's nose of religious bigotry.

Engel's abuses of history were subtly but still powerfully misleading. The Court observed that the First Amendment was meant to outlaw government attempts to "control, support, or influence the kind of prayers the American people can say."[111] "Control" the prayers Americans "can" say? Undoubtedly the First Amendment forestalled that, but nothing in it was understood (until *Engel*) to outlaw all government "influence"—so long as coercion was avoided—upon people *to* pray, even in school. The Court wrote that the Founders knew that "bitter strife" could come when "religious groups struggled with one another to obtain the Government's stamp of approval for each."[112]

This abuse of history should be rejected. The First Amendment, it is true, put the truth of disputed religious matters—doctrine, discipline, worship, church governance—outside the ken of the magistrate. But the Founders accepted the discord that the "multiplicity of sects" created in a free society under God, and affirming voluntarily that there is a God had nothing to do with "sectarian" squabbling.

The *Engel* Court also offered two policy grounds for the "naked public square." The first ground was the claim that anything but the "naked public square" is dangerous to the republic and contributes to the degradation of religion. Is religious belief necessary to good government? Certainly not, replied the *Engel* Court, ringing the sanguinary chimes of religious war that surely, in their view, would erupt if government were involved in supporting religion.

[111.] *Ibid.*, at 429.
[112.] *Ibid.* at 429.

Is religious belief "Necessary to the happiness of mankind"? *Only* where hermetically sealed within an entirely private sphere. The *Engel* Court referred to "unhallowed perversion" of religion by the civil magistrate.[113] To the innocent reader, this might seem to refer to some—perhaps only a small percentage—of all acts by which the state might encourage and promote religion. But, again, the Court argued that religion is "pervert[ed]" whenever the government would touch upon it. History showed, the Court said, that "many people had lost their respect for any religion that had relied upon the support of government to spread its faith."[114] Publicly promoted religion resulted, that is, in a theistic religiosity, if not apostasy.

Justice Tom Clark joined in the *Engel* majority. The following year, he was chosen to write the *Schempp* opinion striking down devotional Bible reading in schools. In a law review article published shortly afterwards, Clark sought to deflect criticism of the Court: "What I say here is by way of what the Court could not say but which needs to be said."

Clark shamelessly waved the bloody cassock. He observed that the terrible consequence of the church–state regime that was *America's* until the day before yesterday needed "no demonstration." He nonetheless mentioned unspecified "bombings of synagogues of a few years ago"; "like occurrences" (again unspecified); and "the Presidential campaign of 1960." This last reference is more than puzzling. The election of the nation's first Catholic President (notwithstanding concerns expressed by many about his "subservience" to Rome) is strong evidence that America's history leads to religious peace rather than to religious strife.

[113.] *Ibid.* at 432.
[114.] *Ibid.* at 431.

School District of Abington Township v. Schempp, 374 U.S. 203 (1963)

Facts of the Case: Pennsylvania law required public schools to begin each day with readings from the Bible and to recite the Lord's Prayer each morning. Students at Abington High School participated in this routine but could be exempted from these exercises by a written note from their parents to the school. Unitarian Church members Edward and Sidney Schempp sued the Abington school district, claming that the mandatory exercises violated the Establishment Clause.

Decision: In an 8-1 decision, the Court ruled that Bible reading and recitation of the Lord's Prayer violated the Establishment Clause.

Majority Opinion: Justice Tom Clark delivered the opinion of the Court, arguing that the Establishment Clause and Free Exercise Clause overlap to prohibit "all legislative power respecting religious belief or the expression thereof." Government, he asserted, must maintain a "neutrality" between religion and non-religion. Justice Clark then laid out a test to apply in Establishment Clause cases: If either the purpose or primary effect of an enactment entails "the advancement or inhibition of religion," it violates the Clause. Thus, in every challenge, the enactment must have "a secular legislative purpose" as well as "a primary effect that neither advances nor inhibits religion."

Concurring Opinion: In a memorable concurrence, Justice William Brennan argued that "[a] too literal quest for the advice of the Founding Fathers upon the issues of these cases seems to me futile and misdirected." Brennan called for interpreting the Religion Clauses of the First Amendment not in light of their original meaning but according to the discernment of the justices in adapting their principles to new circumstances.

Significance: The *Schempp* case demonstrated that the logic of *Everson* would be used to eliminate religion from schools. It also established a strict test that would evolve into the infamous *Lemon* test in *Lemon v. Kurtzman*. This test would be used in many cases to advance secularism.

The most puzzling feature of the whole secularism project launched by the Court in 1962 may be its timing. Never before then could it have been so confidently said that America had achieved a stable religious pluralism. Justice Clark confirmed *Engel's* suggestion that authentic religion decreased just as far as the public realm was infiltrated by God.

Clark made clear that boundary of the secular public realm: Religion was to be wholly private; it belonged *exclusively* to the home, the church, and Sunday school. Most of all, though, Clark anticipated the direction of the Court in his white-hot encomia to religion as "the inviolable citadel of the individual heart and mind"—the sanctuary of the individual.[115] "Present world conditions [again unspecified] make it the more imperative that this sacred right of the individual be fully recognized and equally enforced." He agreed with the proposition that school prayer, for example, retarded rather than promoted real religion—as opposed to conformism.

Besides some more Whig history served up again by Hugo Black, *Engel* is long on assertion and short on reasoning. One may therefore wonder, as we did in analyzing the *Everson* decision: What explains the *Engel* result? Where did *Engel* come from?

Engel quite possibly came from the "new" truth about religion—according to the Court, circa 1962. We have already discussed the corrosive effects of Darwinism, higher criticism, and the Romantics upon traditional belief.[116] By the time the justices published *Engel*, "scientism" had taken a further toll: The methods and tools of the natural sciences produced real (i.e., objective) knowledge; all else was considered to be subjective taste, experience, opinion. Morality had long been under

---

115. *Abington v. Schempp,* 374 U.S. 203, 226.
116. See Chapter 3, *supra.*

siege as a realm of unprovable preference or predilection—
what Oliver Wendell Holmes once famously called a person's
"can't helps." For this reason, and because of the common tie
between morality and people's religious convictions, "religion"
and "morality" seemed to have a common rendezvous: subjec-
tivity, as one's *individuality.*

By 1962, it seems that several of the justices believed that
doctrine, churches, and institutional forms were inimical to
genuine spirituality. Organized religion was the enemy of genuine faith. For them, "orthodoxy" meant "you believe what I
believe and we both believe it because of authority"—hardly
the path to enlightenment or authentic living. The Court
relied at strategic points upon Paul Tillich's "conviction that
religion was, at its essence, a philosophical and theological
'ground of being' whose redefined spiritual centeredness could
successfully confront modern totalitarianism, religious bigotry,
and racism even as it transcended the creedal orthodoxy and
denominational distinctiveness" of traditional religion.[117]

These streams joined in the Court's 1965 opinion in *U.S.
v. Seeger.*[118] The case was about the Selective Service "conscientious objector" provisions for religious believers. The objectors' application for "c.o." status had to be denied because
exemption required an objection, not on the basis of "essentially political, sociological, or philosophical views or a merely
personal moral code," but on the basis of religious "training
and belief" defined as "an individual's belief in a relation to a
Supreme Being involving duties superior to those arising from
any merely human relation."

The *Seeger* Court found that all three objectors merited this
exemption; all were "religious" enough to qualify. The "mod-

[117.]Jon Butler, "Jack-in-the-Box Faith: The Religion Problem in Modern
American History," 70 *J. AM. Hist.* 1357, 1370 (2004).

ern" belief eagerly embraced by a unanimous Court—save for an even more *avant garde* concurrence by William O. Douglas—contrasted sharply with the old view of a "God up there," such as one finds (the Court's example, lifted from a modern theologian) in the Bible. The Court repeated a much older assertion by Douglas (from his 1944 *Ballard* opinion) about the ineffability of religion: "religious experiences which are as real as life to some may be incomprehensible to others." The Court opined that, save for the very few atheists in the universe, "everybody believes in some kind of God," though many do not believe in any transcendent Being capable of communicating duties to human persons. So the *Seeger* Court redefined religion as "belief" or "faith" which, if not in God, occupies in the life of the individual a place parallel to that of God in the lives of the more traditionally religious.

This view of religion was quite different from that of most Americans; it also was certainly different from how the law had viewed religion through the ages. In popular opinion and by tradition in constitutional law, "religion" had to do with a greater than human source of meaning and value—with

---

[118.] *U.S. v. Seeger*, 380 U.S. 163 (1965). The Universal Military Training and Service Act created an exemption for those whose religious belief renders them opposed to military service. To qualify for the "conscientious objector" exemption, one had to have a belief "in relation to a Supreme Being involving duties superior to those arising from any human relation" but excepting "essentially political, sociological, or philosophical views or a merely personal moral code." In short, you had to be a believer to get the exemption rather than having a mere personal, political, or philosophical objection to serving. Seeger and Jackson believed in "supreme reality" or a "universal reality" as the basis for their objection but were not granted the exemption. They sued because they thought that the law unfairly failed to exempt non-religious conscientious objectors. The Court agreed and said that any belief that occupies a central place, like a religious belief, is tantamount to a religious belief.

God. In that tradition, "religion" was contrasted with philosophical, social, and personal political views. One who did not believe in God—an atheist, for example—did not adhere to a religion. For the *Seeger* Court, however, any sincere conviction that "occup[ies]" "the same place" that "belief in God" would hold in the life of an orthodox believer counts as "religious belief."

It is important to note that the *Seeger* Court referred to *beliefs*, not to belief systems, organized communities of believers, or a relationship of any sort, either with others or with a transcendent being or force or principle. That this solitary and untethered belief may be "incomprehensible" to a court or a local draft board made no difference: The objector must be treated as "religious" all the same. The only question was "sincerity": whether the (inscrutable, even nonsensical) belief was "truly held."[119]

What happened starting with *Seeger* seems to be this: Courts subsumed a person's beliefs about a transcendent source of meaning within a wider individual autonomy that is not tethered to faith. "Religion" is just one aspect of a broader freedom of choice whose grounding is not God or what God expects of persons. The new grounding is personal authenticity and the subjective importance of the conviction to the person convinced of it. Justice Arthur Goldberg gave an odd testimony to this development at the justices' *Seeger* conference. "The only difference between Seeger and Buddhism," he observed, "is that Seeger isn't a Buddhist."[120]

Lying also somewhere behind this new view of religion may be the Court's program for social equality without regard to creed, race, gender, sexual preference, etc. The *Seeger* Court

---

[119.] 380 U.S. at 184–185.
[120.] Dickson, ed., *The Supreme Court in Conference*, 436.

looked to Tillich, who looked to Friedrich Schleiermacher. As Tillich wrote in his *Systematic Theology*, those who follow Schleiermacher hold that "experience is the medium through which the sources [creeds, sacred books, and the like] 'speak' to us, through which we receive them."[121] Thus, no ecclesiastical authority—and much less so any principality or power—could settle for *me* what is or is not a valid "experience" of the divine. Religion is therefore not only about the self. It is self-authenticating, and where the *self* authors value, the putative "value judgments" of a political majority cannot plausibly serve to limit anyone's liberty.

This view of liberty—that it is not bound by any moral or legal limits and that each individual can define for himself the meaning of liberty—is explained most strikingly in *Planned Parenthood v. Casey*, the 1992 Supreme Court abortion decision that affirmed *Roe v. Wade*. The Court in *Casey* tied together several lines of cases having to do with legal treatment of marriage, family, and sexual morality. Why, the Court asked, does our law "afford protection to personal decisions relating to marriage, procreation, contraception [and] family relationships?" Not because of any moral truth about marriage, family, or religion. The Court said instead that the common underlying value is personal authenticity. These choices are "central to personal dignity and autonomy." "At the heart of liberty," the Court concluded, "is the right to define one's own concept of existence, of meaning, of the universe, and of the mystery of human life."[122]

---

121. Paul Tillich, *Systematic Theology* (Chicago: University of Chicago Press, 1951), vol.I, 40.

122. *Planned Parenthood of Southeastern Pennsylvania v. Casey*, 505 U.S. 833, at 851.

Chapter 7

THE MODERN COURT'S HOSTILITY TO RELIGION IN EDUCATION

The Supreme Court could not put a stop to student prayers. For one thing, students have private moments during the school day during which they may pray silently. Students are also legally free to get together for group prayer on school premises during non-curricular hours.

More broadly, *Engel* was about *public* schools. These state-run enterprises are open to students of all faiths who attend under the compulsion of truancy laws, though softened by the availability of private schools and the increasing attraction of home-schooling. The holdings and reasoning of the school prayer cases, then, were compatible with state financial assistance to church schools. Such aid had been upheld in *Cochran* and, in effect, in *Everson*. *Zorach* also upheld state aid to religious schools, though not of the financial kind.

The Court's next confrontation with parochial school aid came in 1968 in *Board of Education v. Allen*.[123] The Court's opinion in *Allen* fits neatly within the tradition going back all the way to *Bradfield v. Roberts* (the 1899 case upholding public aid to a hospital run by Catholic Sisters). The *Allen* Court held that the secular education in religious schools was autonomous from religious training. *Allen* also said that the state had a legitimate interest in the competent teaching of nonreligious subjects in parochial schools.

The *Allen* Court never denied that the Catholic schools had an integrated religious mission, although it did not explicitly affirm this either. They were, the opinion for the Court by Justice Byron White repeatedly said, "parochial" schools. But the Court based its analysis not upon the overall mission or identity of the schools, but upon the autonomy of secular training in them. After *Allen*, the way was open for substantial state aid to religious schools, all the way up to the cost of the secular education (alongside religious training) provided in them.

The Court soon blocked the way. The justices struck down a parochial school aid law in the next case they considered, for the first time in the Court's history. The case, *Lemon v. Kurtzman*, was from Pennsylvania. Beginning in *Lemon* (1971), the Supreme Court shifted the focus of its church–state analysis from the public good—secular instruction—provided by parochial schools to the overall "mission" of those schools. At the same time, the Court decided to consider them not simply

---

[123.] *Board of Education v. Allen*, 392 U.S. 236 (1968). A New York law required the state to distribute textbooks to all students in grades seven through 12, regardless of whether they attended public or private school. It did not provide for the distribution of religious textbooks. The Supreme Court upheld the law against an Establishment Clause challenge by saying that the law does not violate "strict separation" of *Everson*: It furthers a secular end and has a secular purpose, so it is not a violation. Importantly, the Court distinguished between the twofold mission of parochial schools: first, secular education and, second, religious education. The Establishment Clause permits government support of the secular mission of parochial schools as long as funds are not spent on religious education.

as private or parochial (as had *Allen*), but as Catholic. This was a new conceptual universe.

Lemon v. Kurtzman, 403 U.S. 602 (1971)

Facts of the Case: Taxpayer Alton J. Lemon challenged state legislation that provided funding for nonpublic religious schools. *Lemon v. Kurtzman* was decided concurrently with *Earley v. DiCenso* (1971) and *Robinson v. DiCenso* (1971), each of which challenged state programs that provided financial support to nonpublic religious schools. Specifically, in Pennsylvania, the 1968 Nonpublic Elementary and Secondary Education Act provided financial support to nonpublic schools for teacher salaries, textbooks, and instructional materials for secular subjects. The Rhode Island Salary Supplement Act of 1969 supplemented 15 percent of salaries for teachers in nonpublic elementary schools.

Decision: In an 8-0 decision, the Court ruled in favor of Lemon that the Pennsylvania and Rhode Island statutes violated the Establishment Clause.

Majority Opinion: Writing for the Court, Chief Justice Warren Burger evaluated the Establishment Clause claim by creating a three-pronged test. The *Lemon* test states that the government's action in question (1) must have a legitimate secular purpose, (2) must not have the primary effect of either advancing or inhibiting religion, and (3) must not result in an "excessive government entanglement" with religion. Both statutes involved a high degree of oversight and involvement with the religious school in order to administer the funding. The Court determined that this high level of involvement led to an excessive entanglement between religion and the state. Since both states' legislation failed the third element of the test, the legislation violated the Establishment Clause.

Significance: *Lemon v. Kurtzman* established the *Lemon* test, which the Court has used (albeit selectively) to determine whether a particular state action violated the Establishment Clause. For legislation to be valid, it must fulfill all three requirements. If even one of the three is not fulfilled, the state's action is a violation of the Establishment Clause.

The abrupt shift in focus was carried through by a fallacious argument. Writing separately for himself in *Lemon*, Justice Brennan expressed the new focal point that was adopted by the Court a few years later (1975) in *Meek v. Pittenger*: "[T]he *secular education* those schools provide goes hand in hand with the *religious mission* which is *the only reason* for the schools' existence. Within the institution, the two are inextricably intertwined" (emphasis added).[124]

Holding this argument together is the assertion that public aid in any amount to any aspect of the curriculum inevitably advances religion in violation of the Constitution. This concept of "pervasively sectarian" served as the linchpin of the Court's entire series of adverse rulings on parochial-school aid from 1971 to 1985. This linchpin is now under fire. A four-justice plurality in *Mitchell v. Helms* said that "hostility to aid to pervasively sectarian schools has a shameful pedigree.... This doctrine, born of bigotry, should be buried now."[125]

---

124. *Meek v. Pittinger*, 421 U.S. 395 (1975). Three separate Pennsylvania laws at issue were challenged as violations of the Establishment Clause. First, a law allowing the states to purchase secular textbooks for private students was upheld under the *Allen* reasoning. Second, a law providing educational materials to parochial schools was struck down as aiding religion. Third, the state's offering of remedial help for special-needs students in private schools was also struck down as aiding religion. Also, the latter provision would require excessive entanglement of government with religion by requiring government to ensure that the teachers are not teaching religion.

125. *Mitchell v. Helms*, 530 U.S. 793 (2000). This is another case involving the loaning of secular educational materials to private schools. Taxpayers challenged the practice as a violation of the Establishment Clause. The Court upheld the practice, stating that government aid to religious schools does not violate the Establishment Clause if the religious teaching cannot be traced to the government aid. In this case, since the government aid involved secular materials, the connection was insufficient to amount to an Establishment Clause violation.

The *Nyquist* decision of 1973 is the most telling of the adverse rulings.[126] In oral argument and in the briefs, those defending New York's aid plan stated flatly that the city's parochial schools were financially *in extremis*. The Court itself recognized that "private schools are confronted with increasingly grave fiscal problems, [and] that resolving these problems by increasing tuition charges forces parents to turn to the public schools."[127]

The situation in *Nyquist* was more urgent because aid was limited to low-income families who would almost certainly be unable to afford private school without public aid. By grants, the "state seeks to relieve [parents'] financial burdens sufficiently to assure that they continue to have the option to send their children to religion-oriented schools." But against our "cherished" "separation of Church from state," the Court said, these appeals counted for little, even though it was clear already (in 1973) that New York's Catholic schools, like those in many other northern cities, were not so much cloisters for white working-class children as alternatives for poorer children—of all religions and races—whose parents wanted them out of undisciplined and ineffective public schools.

[126.] *Committee for Public Education v. Nyquist*, 413 U.S. 756 (1973). A New York law offered grants to nonpublic schools that served a large number of low-income students. The money was given for the maintenance of school facilities. Additionally, low-income parents were given tuition reimbursements. Those parents who failed to qualify for the reimbursements were offered tax deductions for their tuition costs. The legislature wanted to offer all parents a choice in their child's education. The Court found that these grants furthered religion and were therefore unconstitutional. While the aid was not directly to religion (thus seemingly in the line of *Everson*), it furthered religion and therefore violated the Court's Establishment Clause tests.

[127.] 413 U.S. at 795.

The *Nyquist* Court effaced the distinction between aid to the institution and aid to parents, a distinction made in *Everson* that would later be revived by the Court's favorable decision on school vouchers in 2002. The *Nyquist* Court said that grants to parents had the same effect as grants to schools: "to provide desired financial support for nonpublic, sectarian institutions." Either way, they are an "incentive to parents to send their children to sectarian schools," for "the money represents a charge upon the state for the purpose of religious education." The Court concluded that "it is precisely the function of New York's law to provide assistance to private schools, the great majority of which are sectarian." Evidently, the *Nyquist* Court thought the Establishment Clause required them to say that any public spending that helped to keep these schools open was prohibited.

Nyquist established that the "incidental effects" part of the Court's nonestablishment doctrine was elastic enough to rebut any government attempt to funnel money to parochial schools. In a footnote, the Court brushed aside New York's argument that the law's "primary" effect was not to advance religion, but to further education: "We do not think such metaphysical judgments are either possible or necessary." The real test, the Court seemed to say, was whether a challenged program had more than a "remote and incidental effect advantageous to religious institutions."

The pendulum has fortunately swung back toward the Founders' view of church–state cooperation in education. Since the 1985 decisions in *Grand Rapids*[128] and *Aguilar*[129]—cases that represent the furthest extension of the Court's "no-aid" campaign—there has arisen a new (maybe a renewed) appreciation of the singular importance of sound education to success in today's economy; the intractability of underachievement in many public school systems; the educational achievements and liberality of parochial schools; the racial, and even the religious, mix of students in those schools; and the role of choice in education (consider the rise of magnet schools, charter schools, and home schooling). But the pendulum still has a long way to go before we can say that it has come to its proper place.

---

128. *School District of Grand Rapids v. Ball*, 473 U.S. 373 (1985). This case involved two separate programs that were challenged as violations of the Establishment Clause. The first, a shared-time program, provided supplemental classes to parochial schools in religious school classrooms. The second, a community education program, was an after-hours program meant to teach religious school students on religious school property, also with taxpayer money. The Court invalidated both programs because their primary effect was to further or advance religion in violation of the *Lemon* test.

129. *Aguilar v. Felton*, 473 U.S. 402 (1985). In this case, New York City used Title I of the Elementary and Secondary Education Act of 1965 to reimburse the salaries of public employees who supplied remedial teaching services to low-income parochial school students. The Court invalidated this practice as a violation of the Establishment Clause because it fostered state–church entanglement in violation of the *Lemon* test due to the oversight role the city was forced to play in ensuring that the education paid for by the public is secular in nature.

Chapter 8

CONFUSION AND CONTRADICTION IN THE TWO RELIGION CLAUSES

*T*he second school prayer case—*Schempp*—was decided in 1963. During the same term, the Court's decision in *Sherbert v. Verner* sent a seemingly contrary signal about religion and public life. In *Sherbert*, the Court interpreted the Free Exercise Clause to prohibit the government from imposing "burdens" on acts motivated by a "sincere" religious belief, save where the government can show that the burden is the "least restrictive" means available to serve a "compelling interest." The basic posture conveyed by this test is a sharp contrast to that of *Engel* and *Schempp*. *Sherbert* seems to be an affirmation of religion, a strong judicial endorsement of faith over law; *Engel* represents the triumph, it is alleged, of politics over religion.

These appearances are deceiving. The *Sherbert* doctrine never yielded many decrees of relief for believers, and there is good reason to believe that it was never meant to do so. The immediate effect of *Sherbert* doctrine was to clothe the courts with authority to police the boundary between government power and individual prerogative. This is just where the Court wanted to sit: as American society's church–state ombudsman. In fact, *Sherbert* stands with *Engel* for the proposition that legislators (and, in turn, the people) cannot be trusted to handle religion.

Sherbert v. Verner, 374 U.S. 398 (1963)

Facts of the Case: Adeil Sherbert, a member of the Seventh-day Adventist Church, was fired from her job after she refused to work on Saturday, the Sabbath Day of her faith. The South Carolina Employment Security Commission did not accept her justification for refusing to work on Saturday and accordingly denied her unemployment benefits. Sherbert claimed that this denial of benefits violated her right to free exercise of religion.

Decision: In a 7-2 decision, the Court determined that failing to provide unemployment benefits violated her right to free exercise of religion.

Majority Opinion: Writing for the majority, Justice William Brennan argued that disqualifying Sherbert from receiving benefits imposed a burden on her free exercise of religion. Sherbert would have had to choose between the benefits and her religious tenets. The state claimed that it denied Sherbert benefits to serve a compelling state interest in preventing fraudulent claims for benefits. Although the government may infringe upon the free exercise right in service of a compelling state interest, the Court determined that the state's compelling interest was not serious enough to limit the free exercise rights of citizens.

Significance: The Court created the *Sherbert* test to balance free exercise claims and governmental action. The *Sherbert* test has two parts. First, the individual claiming free exercise violation must hold a "sincere religious belief" that is significantly burdened by state action. Second, if the state burdens the sincere belief, then the government must prove that it has a "compelling state interest" and that the means of pursuing that interest are narrowly tailored to be least burdensome to religion.

Sherbert broke decisively with the whole tradition of judicial interpretation of the Free Exercise Clause. It was a short-lived experiment: In 1990, the Court reversed itself in the case of *Employment Division of Oregon v. Smith. Oregon v. Smith* was a case where two counselors at a drug rehabilitation clinic were fired and declared ineligible for unemployment benefits because of "work-related misconduct." They had violated a contractual provision requiring them to remain absolutely drug-free by ingesting peyote (a hallucinogen containing mescaline) at a Native American religious ceremony. Such conduct was also contrary to Oregon criminal law; peyote ingestion was generally prohibited, and Oregon, unlike the federal government as well as 23 other states, did not specifically exempt its sacramental use from the general prohibition.

The *Smith* Court held that courts had no authority under the Free Exercise Clause to exempt anyone from generally applicable laws that were neutral about religion. The Court said that the Free Exercise Clause did prohibit laws aimed at religion in the specific sense we have encountered here and there in this book: where a strictly religious motive or belief or presupposition is singled out by the lawmaker as false or invalid. After *Smith*, the Free Exercise Clause would prohibit a zoning law that banned the use of single-family homes for religious assemblies but not for pool parties or other similarly large social gatherings.

The *Smith* Court spent most of its time arguing against one interpretation of the Free Exercise Clause: the conduct exemption. But without identifying it as such, and without historical argument, the Court came close to expressing the meaning apprehended by the ratifiers:

> [A]ssembling with others for a worship service, participating in sacramental use of bread and wine, proselytizing, abstaining from certain foods or certain modes of transportation.... [A] state would be "prohibiting the free exercise [of

religion]" if it sought to ban such acts...*only* when they are engaged in for religious reasons, or only because of the religious belief that they display.

Employment Division of Oregon v. Smith, 494 U.S. 872 (1990)

Facts of the Case: Alfred Smith and Galen Black were fired from their jobs with a private drug rehabilitation organization because they ingested peyote—a hallucinogenic drug—for sacramental purposes at a ceremony of the Native American Church, of which both were members. The State of Oregon determined that Smith and Black were ineligible for unemployment compensation because they were fired for work-related "misconduct." Black and Smith claimed that the denial of unemployment benefits violated their free exercise rights.

Decision: In a 6-3 decision, the Court determined that the Employment Division of Oregon's denial of unemployment benefits did not violate Smith and Black's right to the free exercise of religion.

Majority Opinion: Writing for the majority, Justice Antonin Scalia rejected the compelling governmental interest test applied in *Sherbert.* Instead, Scalia argued that the claim of free exercise of religion does not exempt one from a neutral, generally applicable law, such as the law Smith and Black violated that forbade drug use. In limited cases, the legislature may grant an accommodation that exempts religious practice from a generally applicable law. Smith and Black did not have a presumptive right to an accommodation. Moreover, the Court did not have the authority to exempt practices from generally applicable laws.

Significance: In previous cases dealing with religious liberty and unemployment benefits, such as *Sherbert v. Verner,* the Court used a balancing test to determine whether the compelling governmental interest justified denying unemployment benefits. In *Smith,* the Court rejected the compelling governmental interest test, arguing that the claim of free exercise does not presumptively exempt one from neutral, generally applicable laws.

The decisive feature is not the conduct exemption's "neutrality of effect," but rather what might be called "neutrality of reasons." John Locke provided a useful illustration, albeit long before the founding of the Constitution and a very long time before *Smith*:

> [I]f any people congregated upon account of religion should be desirous to sacrifice a calf, I deny that that ought to be prohibited by a law. Meliboeus, whose calf it is, may lawfully kill his calf at home, and burn any part of it that he thinks fit. For no injury is thereby done to any one, no prejudice to another man's goods. And for the same reason he may kill his calf also in a religious meeting. Whether the doing so be well pleasing to God or not, it is their part to consider that do it.... But if peradventure such were the state of things that the interest of the commonwealth required all slaughter of beasts should be forborne for some while, in order to the increasing of the stock of cattle that had been destroyed by some extraordinary murrain, who sees not that the magistrate, in such a case, may forbid all his subjects to kill any calves for any use whatsoever? Only 'tis to be observed, that in this case the law is not made about a religious, but a political matter; nor is the sacrifice, but the slaughter of calves, thereby prohibited.[130]

The Supreme Court later (1993) applied the principle to a Hialeah, Florida, ordinance that seemingly was directed at

---

[130.] John Locke, "A Letter Concerning Toleration," in Locke, *The Second Treatise on Government and A Letter Concerning Toleration*, 147–148 (J. Gough, ed., 1976).

the Santeria sect (evidently, a Caribbean blend of Christian and folk beliefs) that forbade the ritual slaughter of animals. The constitutional issue was that the law did not prohibit animal slaughter for sport or food. The Court correctly struck down the law, following *Smith*.[131]

Church of Lukumi Babalu Aye v. City of Hialeah, 508 U.S. 520 (1993)

Facts: The Church of Lukumi Babalu Aye practiced Santeria, which uses animal sacrifice as a form of worship. The City Council in Hialeah, Florida, adopted several ordinances prohibiting animal sacrifice and animal slaughter. Since the law exempted certain forms of animal killing, the members of the church claimed that the ordinances violated their right to free exercise of religion.

Decision: In a 9-0 vote, the Court ruled in favor of the Church of Lukumi Babalu Aye, agreeing that the ordinances violated the Church's free exercise right.

Majority Opinion: The Hialeah law forbade animal sacrifice but allowed hunters, butchers, and restaurants to kill animals for non-religious uses. Functionally, the law targeted Santeria worship alone. The city claimed a compelling governmental interest in protecting public health and preventing animal cruelty. Yet, since the city had outlawed one form of animal slaughter rather than all animal slaughter, the compelling governmental interest failed.

Significance: In the same way that free exercise does not exempt one from neutral, generally applicable law, laws cannot be crafted specifically to outlaw a religious practice.

Justice Scalia rightly opined in *Smith* that the Free Exercise Clause was a "negative" protection in that the scope of judicially enforceable exemptions (such as in *Hialeah*) was impor-

---

[131.]See *Church of Lukumi Babalu Aye v. City of Hialeah,* 508 U.S. 520 (1993).

tant but limited. Legislation could greatly expand, he said, upon this "negative" protection: "[A] society that believes in the negative protection accorded to religious belief can be expected to be solicitous of that value in its legislation as well." Except that the modern Court's interpretation of the Establishment Clause stands in the way. More exactly, the Court's doctrines forbade any preference or aid for religion. According to the Supreme Court, non-establishment entails strict neutrality between belief and unbelief. Under no circumstances may public authority "endorse" (the Court's word) religion as a good thing.

"What a strange notion," Scalia wrote in 1993, "that a Constitution which *itself* gives 'religion in general' preferential treatment (I refer to the Free Exercise Clause) forbids endorsement of religion in general."[132] It is strange indeed that the Court has put the Establishment and Free Exercise Clauses on a collision course.

The strangest collision occurred in *Thornton v. Caldor, Inc.*, at the 1985 high-water mark of the Court's privatization campaign.[133] At issue was a Connecticut law stating that "No person who states that a particular day of the week is observed as his Sabbath may be required by his employer to work on such

---

[132.] *Lamb's Chapel v. Center Moriches Union Free School District*, 508 U.S. 384 (1993), at 400. Emphasis in original.

[133.] *Estate of Thornton v. Caldor, Inc.*, 472 U.S. 703 (1985). Thornton was demoted from a managerial position to a clerical position because of his refusal to work on the Sabbath. Connecticut law stated that no person who states that a particular day of the week is his Sabbath can be required to work on that day and that his refusal to work on that day will not be grounds for dismissal. The Supreme Court heard his estate's case and determined that the Connecticut law violated the Establishment Clause because its primary effect is to advance religion. Thus, it could not be used as a defense of Thornton's refusal to work on the Sabbath.

day. An employee's refusal to work on his Sabbath shall not constitute grounds for his dismissal."

Thornton had been demoted from a managerial position at a Caldor store for refusing to work on his Sabbath—Sunday. But the statute was scrupulously neutral among religions: Not only the "Lord's Day," but any day at all qualified for the same treatment, provided it was someone's "Sabbath." Because *Sherbert v. Verner* held that the Free Exercise Clause protects Sabbatarians against disqualification for unemployment benefits, there was surely enough reason to expect that Thornton would prevail.

The Court invalidated the Connecticut law as a violation of "neutrality" and concluded that the law "impermissibly advances a particular religious practice" and thus violates the Establishment Clause. The Court claimed that this law discriminated against unbelief. The law gave "Sabbath observers the valuable right to designate a particular weekly day off—typically a [widely prized] weekend day," but "other employees who have strong and legitimate, but non-religious reasons for wanting a weekend day off have no rights under the statute."

Justice David Souter's opinion (for Justices Sandra Day O'Connor and John Paul Stevens) in a 1992 public school graduation prayer case, *Lee v. Wiseman*, is an attempt to resolve this contradiction between accommodations for believers and the Establishment Clause. Souter wanted to justify special "accommodation" of religious believers. He opined that "accommodation" of believers without equal concern for the irreligious was constitutionally acceptable because "accommodation" showed only "respect" for religion. He distinguished a permitted "respect" from a prohibited "endorsement" of religion.

"Respect," Souter continued, allows us "to act without expressing a position on the theological merit of those values. . . ." Fair enough: We do not necessarily affirm the truth of any Islamic tenets when we say that Muslims have a right to religious worship. But Souter then added, ". . .or on the merits of religious belief in general." Souter is back where he began: On what basis do we act in some special way to respect or accommodate specifically religious practices without endorsing religion? How do we respect religion completely apart from any judgment about the value of religion?

The Supreme Court's struggle to reconcile constitutional directions to make no distinction between religion and nonreligion, yet to accord religion "free exercise" accommodations, continued in the 2005 case upholding the Religious Land Use and Institutionalized Persons Act (RLUIPA). Enacted in 2000, this statute was a partial revival by Congress of the judicially abandoned balancing test of *Sherbert v. Verner*. An Ohio prison inmate (an "institutionalized person") complained in the language of RLUIPA that his "nonmainstream" Satanist religion was "burden[ed]" by the warden's denying him and his co-religionists various privileges granted to other religions.

The problem created by Establishment Clause doctrine was this: Religious prisoners were singled out by RLUIPA for beneficial treatment that inmates wishing to gather for non-religious purposes were denied. Imagine that a group of Klansmen could not meet to discuss their racist doctrines, but the same men describing themselves now as members of an Aryan church might be able to do so. Even if the warden said no to the Aryan church, there is no doubt that RLUIPA gave its members a chance to go to court that the Klansmen did not have.

The lower appellate court held in favor of the warden: RLUIPA "impermissibly advanc[es] religion by giving greater protection to religious rights than to other constitutionally protected rights." Doing so might "encourage" religious belief among prisoners, and that would not comport with the Establishment Clause's strict command that (according to the Court's current doctrine) government not favor or promote religion—or "endorse" it in any way—over and against non-religion. Belief and unbelief must be absolutely on par.

On appeal, the Supreme Court in *Cutter v. Wilkinson* recognized the difficulty of "accommodating" religion without "fostering" it.[134] It said that the two clauses "exert conflicting pressures" and are "frequently in tension." It acknowledged, too, that there were "shoals" in prior cases but argued that there was a "corridor" through which RLUIPA might slip: "'[N]eutrality' is not so narrow a channel that the slightest deviation from an absolutely straight course leads to condemnation." There is sufficient "play in the joints" for RLUIPA.

Even so, the Court never used the word "endorsement," nor did it explain just how the "corridor"—no matter how "narrow"—could open at all without some distinction between religion and non-religion. The Court observed correctly that other accommodations would be imperiled by a

---

[134.] *Cutter v. Wilkinson*, 544 U.S. 709 (2005). The Religious Land Use and Institutionalized Persons Act prohibited government from imposing a substantial burden on prisoners' free exercise of religion. A burden could be justified if the government showed that it furthered a "compelling government interest" and employed "the least restrictive means" to burden the prisoner's free exercise. Convicts in an Ohio prison claimed that prison officials violated the law by not allowing them to practice their religion. The prison officials countered that accommodating the prisoners' free exercise of religion would amount to a state endorsement of religion that runs afoul of the Establishment Clause. In a unanimous decision, the Court ruled that the law did not violate the Establishment Clause by requiring state prison officials to accommodate prisoners' free exercise of religion. While the Court acknowledged that at some point, "accommodation may devolve into an unlawful fostering of religion," in this case the accommodation fell within the "play in the joints between" the Free Exercise and Establishment Clauses.

strict application of "endorsement" analysis (such as in *Caldor*), but that is to point to the tension, not to resolve it.

The Court also said that RLUIPA could be viewed not as endorsing religion, but as removing a government-imposed burden. Perhaps, but the question remains: May government remove *only* burdens on religion, leaving them upon others, without making a forbidden distinction?

The practical effect of this avoidance was a narrow construction of the narrow channel: "Should inmate requests for religious accommodation become excessive, impose unjustified burdens on other institutionalized persons, or jeopardize the effective functioning of an institution, the facility would be free to resist the imposition."

Chapter 9

A TALE OF TWO TABLETS

On June 27, 2005, the Supreme Court passed judgment on the Ten Commandments. In two cases decided by five-to-four votes, the Court held that the government may— and may not—display the Decalogue.

In one case, two Kentucky counties violated the Constitution by posting the Commandments on interior courthouse walls. These Ten Commandments did not stand alone. They were arrayed with other celebrated documents, including the Declaration of Independence, Magna Carta, Bill of Rights, and Mayflower Compact, all indicative of the Founders' understanding: natural religion, objective morality secured by religion, the "missing *Federalist Paper.*" Passing viewers were advised that the documents all had to do with the moral foundations of our Republic. It was reasonably clear, too, that they all illustrated, in one way or another, that the ethical monotheism we find in the Bible anchored that foundation.

The Supreme Court in *McCreary County v. ACLU* was openly skeptical of the county authorities' motives and aims.[135] The majority speculated that some officials were really just "reaching for any way to keep a religious document on the walls of courthouses." (The Court supposed that doing so was obviously unconstitutional.)

These justices did not deny that ethical monotheism is central to understanding and appreciating our form of government and laws. They critically questioned—but never denied—that the nine documents displayed evidenced ethical monotheism. Thus, these justices reached this paradoxical holding: It *could* be—and, for argument's sake, it *is*—true that our Republic is founded upon ethical monotheism such as we find in the Bible, but saying so on the courthouse walls would violate the religious "neutrality" on which our Republic was founded.

That same June day, the Supreme Court decided that Texas may display the Ten Commandments outside the state capitol.[136] This "monolith" (the Court's word) was ten times bigger than the document posted on the Kentucky courthouse walls.

The state argued that the surrounding 16 "monuments" and score of "markers" commemorated the "people, ideals and events that compose Texan identity." But none of the other "monuments" was religious in tone or appearance. Almost all were reminders of martial exploits. There were monuments to the Alamo, Hood's Brigade, Confederate veterans, the Texas Rangers, a Texas cowboy, the Texas National Guard, and veterans of the nation's other wars. (There was also a monument to "Pioneer Women" and another to "Texas School Children.") The state capitol display was thus very largely a unified set of

---

[135.] *McCreary County v. ACLU,* 545 U.S. 844 (2005). The American Civil Liberties Union sued two Kentucky counties for displaying the Ten Commandments within larger displays of historical documents in courthouses and public schools. The ACLU alleged that these displays violated the Establishment Clause. The Court agreed on the grounds that the Kentucky counties' purpose was to advance religion, pointing to the fact that the counties had deliberately looked for a way to validate the displays of the Ten Commandments by including them in larger displays.

military remembrances and a few unrelated monuments, of which the Decalogue was one.

Four members of the majority in *Van Orden v. Perry*, including Justices Scalia, Clarence Thomas, and Anthony Kennedy and Chief Justice Rehnquist, said (as they said in *McCreary*) that government "[r]ecognition of the role of God in our Nation's heritage" was fitting. Displaying the Decalogue acknowledged that "our institutions presuppose a Supreme Being." And that was good enough. For these four justices, there was no need for Texas to say that the many documents had a common non-religious theme, as Kentucky had said (to no avail) in *McCreary*. For these justices, the Constitution countenanced government affirmation of natural religion and an objective morality packaged with it. These justices were, of course, right.

The four *Van Orden* dissenters, who included Justices Ruth Bader Ginsburg, Souter, Stevens, and O'Connor, said much the same that they, too, said in *McCreary*. The Decalogue monument conveyed a clearly religious message, and that message violated the constitutional command of "neutrality," just as

---

136. See *Van Orden v. Perry*, 545 U.S. 677 (2005). In a case remarkably similar to the *McCreary County* case, a display of the Ten Commandments within a larger display of Texas' historical and cultural heritage was upheld by the Court against a challenge that the display of the Ten Commandments violated the Establishment Clause. The plurality opinion of the Court reasoned that America's history and tradition supported such public displays of religious signs and that, when dealing with state actions grounded in history and tradition, "[s]imply having religious content or promoting a message consistent with a religious doctrine does not run afoul of the Establishment Clause." The plurality qualified its opinion, however, by saying that "[t]here are, of course, limits to the display of religious messages or symbols" and pointing to the fact that in other instances the Court has not been reluctant to strike down practices that evince intent to advance religion.

did the *McCreary* documents, only even more so: The Texas monuments and markers were a motley assortment that did nothing to neutralize the endorsement of natural religion, which any observer would infer from such conspicuous display of the Commandments.

Justice Souter said in his *Van Orden* dissent that incorporating the Decalogue into an "exposition" of its influence on "modern law" would "most likely" be unobjectionable. But the rough treatment these justices gave the Kentucky display suggests otherwise.

Justice Stephen Breyer was the variable, the "swing" vote. He agreed in *McCreary* that an "objective observer" could see only a "religious" purpose behind nine documents, one of which was the Decalogue, so he voted to overturn the displays. In *Van Orden*, however, he said that the stand-alone monument conveyed to the observer a "mixed but primarily non-religious purpose." The "monolith" fell, in Breyer's judgment, on the permissible side of the constitutional line.

He could not explain why, however. Breyer confessed that he was perplexed by this "borderline" case at the far end of legal tests and doctrines. The case was very "fact-intensive," insusceptible to "formulaic" resolution. The monument was "as a practical matter of *degree*...unlikely to prove divisive" (emphasis in original). This matter of "degree" was "critical in a borderline case." Resolution of this vexing question called for raw "legal judgment," a form of discernment not to be confused with "personal judgment." The Decalogue stands or falls for Breyer as obscenity did for Justice Potter Stewart in *Miller v. California*. In a concurring opinion in that case, Stewart confessed that he could not define obscenity, but he insisted, "I know it when I see it." Similarly, Breyer admitted he could not draw a bright line between displays that violate the First

Amendment and displays that are acceptable, but he knew a violation when he saw it.

Chief Justice Rehnquist said in *Van Orden* that the two cases illustrate the "Januslike" quality of Establishment Clause cases. "One face looks toward the strong role played by religion and religious traditions throughout our Nation's history." The "other face," Rehnquist said, "looks toward the principle that governmental intervention in religious matters can itself endanger religious freedom."

In *McCreary*, the Court affirmed the master principle of judge-made constitutional law for the past 40 years: no government promotion or encouragement of religion. Public authority must never "endorse" religion. To do so would say or imply that religion is, in some way or sense, good or desirable as compared to "irreligion." Any such favorable comparison would violate the constitutional command of "neutrality," which requires that the government never endorse religion lest those who are not religious perceive themselves to be "outsiders" or "second-class citizens"—somehow not *equal*.

If, however, there is thought to be an objective common good in religion, as the Founders surely believed there was, then everyone benefits from its public sustenance. Moreover, once the public's perception of religion is lowered, the perception of an individual observer becomes the wild card of church–state constitutional law.

The no-endorsement rule was qualified in a very limited way in *Van Orden*. Government's otherwise strictly taboo relationship with religion may be relaxed where, but only where, "religion" may be grasped under a non-religious heading. Justice Breyer said the Decalogue conveyed "primarily" a "non-religious" message about history. The other majority justices refer to the role of religion in our tradition and the displays as recognition thereof—and not recognition of religion as such, straight-on, as itself something good. In other contexts, the Court has tolerated token acknowledgments that we are a "religious people whose institutions presuppose a Supreme Being" by calling them "ceremonial deism"—"In God We Trust" on currency and (maybe) "under God" in the Pledge of Allegiance.

The Court's 2005 defense of its secularist master principle cases rested upon two conceptually distinct arguments. One is history, chiefly that of the Founding. The second argument is the more interesting: What do the times—*our* times, that is—require as the Justices see it? This second justification is prescriptive, not descriptive. It is frankly normative. It does not rely upon the authority of the Framers, but upon the insights and remedies on offer from the Court. This second defense proceeds from a candid account of the role of religion in our public realm as dangerous and divisive and from the argument that religious liberty does not depend upon public encouragement and support of religion.

Divisiveness is once more a central theme. As early as *Everson*, the justices had begun to turn Madison upside down. Whereas James Madison in *Federalist* No. 10 studiously described how our political system could safely accommodate sectarian friction—and how the alternatives were far worse than his calculated remedy—the modern Court surrenders our politics at first sight (or apparition) of the bloody surplice.

The modern Court's emphasis on the divisiveness of religion was again a theme in *McCreary*. The *McCreary* Court wrote that the "Framers and the citizens of their time intended not only to protect the integrity of individual conscience in religious matters." They also aimed to "guard against the civic divisiveness that follows when the government weighs in on one side of a religious debate."[137] The Court characteristically reached back beyond the Founding for a cogent historical lesson: "We are centuries away from the St. Bartholomew's Day Massacre and the treatment of heretics in early Massachusetts," the Court warned in June 2005, but "the divisiveness of religion in current public life is inescapable."

Neither in *McCreary* nor in any earlier case did the Court supply evidence of the cited strain on our politics. Who knew that the lessons of such distant history were still so stark?

The *McCreary* majority conceded that the thinking of the "framing generation" was demonstrably at odds with their own. "Justice Story reflected" the Founders' thinking when he said that the purpose of the Establishment Clause was not to put all religions on an equal footing but to "exclude all rivalry among Christian sects." True enough, but the Establishment Clause does not actually refer to "sects," much less only to "Christian sects." It refers to "religion." The Establishment Clause was articulated in a world populated almost exclusively by the various Christian churches, but it extended by its language to all belief systems that are, in reality, "religio[us]." The Founders could not have known anything about Mormonism, Christian Science, Jehovah's Witnesses, or the Seventh Day Adventists. They nonetheless described a class of phenomena—religions—into which these 19th century movements can all be comfortably fit.

The *McCreary* majority offered a grotesquely inadequate pair of alternatives: Either adhere to the Founders' limited "purpose" of bringing peace among Christians or submit to "applications unanticipated by the Framers." Grab the former horn of the dilemma, and one must draw the unpalatable outcome that non-Christian believers are outsiders to the Constitution according to the majority's reasoning. The Court invites the reader by default to accept its handiwork; but in doing so,

---

[137.] *McCreary County v. ACLU*, 545 U.S. 844, at 876.

the justices beg the main question: Why should the *McCreary* majority's "application" be the only one worth considering? Why not follow the principles and practice of the Founders?

CONCLUSION

*T*he privatization project launched by *Engel* crested in
1985. Since then, some advances have been made in
bringing religion back into the public square, where the
Founders claimed it belonged from the beginning of the
republic.

For one thing, public forums are now open to religious
expression just as they are open to non-religious speech. Cases
beginning in 1993 with *Lamb's Chapel*[138] and 1995 with
Rosenberger[139] have all but eradicated discrimination against
religious speech, institutions, and individuals as, or on the
precise grounds of being, religious. Where the religious

[138.] *Lamb's Chapel v. Center Moriches Union Free School District,* 508 U.S. 384
(1993). Pursuant to a New York law authorizing school districts to
regulate the use of facilities after school hours, the Center Moriches
School District adopted rules that permitted the use of its facilities
after hours for social, civic, and recreational purposes. However, the
district also adopted a rule that prohibited any group from using its
facilities for religious purposes. Lamb's Chapel applied for permission
to use the district's facilities and was denied. The Court sided with
Lamb's Chapel on the grounds that the district's decision to deny its
facilities to Lamb's Chapel was motivated by the particular viewpoint
of the religious group. This, the Court judged, was a violation of the
right to free speech, which mandates that restrictions must be "viewpoint neutral." Moreover, the Court claimed that permitting Lamb's
Chapel to use its facilities would not violate the Establishment Clause
because it would preserve a strict neutrality, giving Lamb's Chapel
only an equal and neutral opportunity to present its viewpoint alongside other competing viewpoints.

activity (or speech or writing) can be counted among a set of activities that includes non-religion members, then the public forum must be given equal religious time. If a local public library sets up a lecture series on "family issues," it may not exclude a speaker (such as Dr. James Dobson) because he brings a religious perspective to the subject. Or, if a public university subsidizes "student newspapers," it may not exclude from its largesse student newspapers published by, say, the Intervarsity Christian Fellowship.

This was a real breakthrough. *Engel's* legacy prominently included the notion that religion was uniquely problematic politically. Because religion fostered divisiveness and oppression, the state had to keep it private, or else endless problems would ensue. All sorts of political and ideological messages could be heard at high school assemblies and graduations. Even the faintest echoes of the sacred had to be excluded.

Convictions about the unique dangers of public religiosity have not disappeared from the cases, as we saw with the 2005 Decalogue decisions, but fear of mixing religion and politics is waning both on and off the courts in America. However, it is important to note that though the *Lamb's Chapel/Rosenberger*

[139.] *Rosenberger v. Rector and Visitors of the University of Virginia*, 515 U.S. 819 (1995). Ronald Rosenberger requested funds from a student activities fund to defray publication costs of a religious publication. The university refused to provide funds because it promotes religious belief or belief in a fundamental reality. The Supreme Court ruled that this was a violation of the First Amendment's Free Speech clause because the university imposed viewpoint discrimination against Rosenberger's religious beliefs and imposed a financial burden on Rosenberger's speech. Also, the Court ruled that providing the funds to Rosenberger would not amount to a violation of the Establishment Clause because it would only require the university to fund religious materials equally with materials promoting an atheistic viewpoint, thus preserving the precedents that require government neutrality between religion and irreligion.

breakthrough is very important, and though it has been fueled by reduced judicial hostility to religion, it was decided as Free Speech and Free Press doctrine, not on the basis of the Religion Clauses. Establishment Clause doctrine remains "neutrality" between religion and "non-religion."

What might be called "pure" religious expression—speech and acts that have no non-religious analogue—has been rendered bereft of constitutional protection by the Court. Worship, prayer, and proselytizing are examples of uniquely religious speech-acts. Though each could perhaps be described in non-religious terms (assemblies for performances or advocacy speech), it is better to view them as irreducibly and distinctively religious. They are. What is wrong with the Court's approach to these issues is therefore not the characterization of them as "pure" religion. The problem is that the Court's "no-aid" Establishment Clause norm forbids all public support of these activities. Besides, there is no possibility of government neutrality between belief and unbelief when it comes to these kinds of speech-acts, for there is no analogue in the unbeliever's world to worship or other examples of speech-acts.

Another recent sign of positive change is the Court's unanimous 2005 decision in *Cutter v. Wilkinson*.[140] The constitutional challenge to the federal Religious Land Use and Institutionalized Persons Act was essentially that the law gave preferential treatment to believers over non-believers. In fact, RLUIPA did indeed seek to ease the burden of believers caught in the maws of zoning and prison authorities. According to the law, a church or mission chapel could not be "zoned" out where, at least sometimes, a comparably sized Odd Fellows Hall or supper club could be; and in every case,

---

[140.] 544 U.S. 709 (2005).

the church was entitled to strict judicial scrutiny, which was unavailable to the Odd Fellows and other secular institutions.

The Supreme Court declared that this preference was not unconstitutional. Where congressional favors of this sort are concerned (state solicitude is a different matter), the constitutional law has long been, as Professor Carl Esbeck recently wrote, that such preferences do not run afoul of the Establishment Clause.[141] (Another example of such favors is the allowance within employment discrimination laws for churches to discriminate on the grounds of faith when filling "mission-oriented" positions.) The *Cutter* court fell into line with this tradition—a tradition that belies, as far as it goes, strict neutrality between religion and "non-religion."

Still another important recent development in constitutional law has to do with aid to religious schools. The Court struck down a parochial school aid law for the first time in 1971, in *Lemon v. Kurtzman.* The most stringent of these decisions was *Committee for Public Education v. Nyquist,*[142] handed down in 1973. The last Supreme Court holding against a law aiding parochial schools occurred in 1985. Since then, the Court has sustained all parochial challenges that it has heard, trimming back the unfortunate three-part *Lemon* test along the way.

The overall picture of our constitutional law with respect to church and state in contemporary times is this: Free Exercise doctrine is just about where it should be. It should be where the Founders put it, and *Oregon v. Smith* accomplished that. Establishment Clause doctrine is still fundamentally mistaken. It should not mandate neutrality between religion and non-religion. Yet according to the Court's long-standing doctrines, it does. Though the effects of the Court's "no aid at

---

[141.] C. Esbeck, "'Play in the Joints Between the Religious Clauses' and Other Supreme Court Catecheses," 34 *Hofstra L. Rev.* (2006).
[142.] 413 U.S. 756 (1973).

all" stricture have softened recently, especially where public funds are channeled to religious institutions, either indirectly (vouchers) or directly (charitable choice), the law remains basically where *Engel* put it.

What are the prospects now for overruling *Engel's* secularist decree? There are only two announced votes on the present Court for restoration of the Founders' understanding of the Establishment Clause. Justice Scalia said in *Lamb's Chapel*[143] that the Constitution requires that aid to religion not discriminate among faiths. Otherwise, the aid is constitutionally fine. On the assumption that Chief Justice John Roberts and Justice Samuel Alito will make common cause with Thomas and Scalia, Anthony Kennedy becomes the decisive variable.

Will Kennedy supply the needed fifth vote to reject finally the secularism that has squatted in the public square since 1962? It is impossible to say. Kennedy has never been a "strict separationist." He joined key parts of the vigorous dissent written by Scalia in *McCreary*, and that dissent was highly critical not only of the majority's holding in *McCreary*, but also of the whole doctrinal patrimony generated by *Lemon v. Kurtzman*.

Of course, no change for the better in Establishment Clause doctrine would *require* government support of religion. The Founders believed fervently that religion and morality were essential to republican government. Yet even they did not constitutionally mandate state aid or encouragement. They permitted and expected it. As legislators they enacted it. But the governing constitutional principle was captured in the Northwest Ordinance: Schools and the means of education should forever be "encouraged."

Americans today would meet that expectation. Today there is a popular conviction, similar to the Founders' view,

---

143. 508 U.S. at 397–401 (Scalia, J., and Thomas, J., concurring).

that religion can contribute mightily to solving social ills, to good government, and to mankind's happiness.

In his *Everson* dissent, Justice Rutledge said that "no provision of the Constitution is more closely tied to or given content by its generating history than the religious clause of the First Amendment."[144] Yet just one year later in *McCollum*, Justice Jackson, who did not disagree with Rutledge on the merits of either *Everson* or *McCollum*, opined that key Establishment Clause issues are matters "on which we can find no law but our own prepossessions."[145] Justice White concluded in 1973 that courts have "carved out what they deemed to be the most desirable national policy governing various aspects of church-state relationships."[146]

Justice White was right: Privatization has been a judicial policy experiment. Born in 1962, the privatization project has been in decline for almost two decades. With a little more time and a little more experience, we may be able to judge it a clumsy but plausible transition to what the Justices for a time could scarcely imagine: religious liberty in a pluralistic society—one in which government has the constitutional authority to aid and promote religion and does so.

---

144. 330 U.S. I, 33 (Rutledge dissenting)

145. 333 U.S. 203, 238 (Jackson, J., concurring)

146. *Committee for Public Education & Religious Liberty v. Nyquist*, 413 U.S. 756, 820 (1973) (White, J., dissenting).

ABOUT THE AUTHOR

Gerard V. Bradley is Professor of Law at the University of Notre Dame and the Director of the Witherspoon Institute's Center on Religion and the Constitution. He has published extensively in the areas of constitutional law, religion, and public life. His books include *Church–State Relationships in America* (Greenwood Press, 1987); *A Student's Guide to the Study of Law* (Intercollegiate Studies Institute, 2006); and *Essays on Law, Religion and Morality* (University of Scranton Press, 2007).